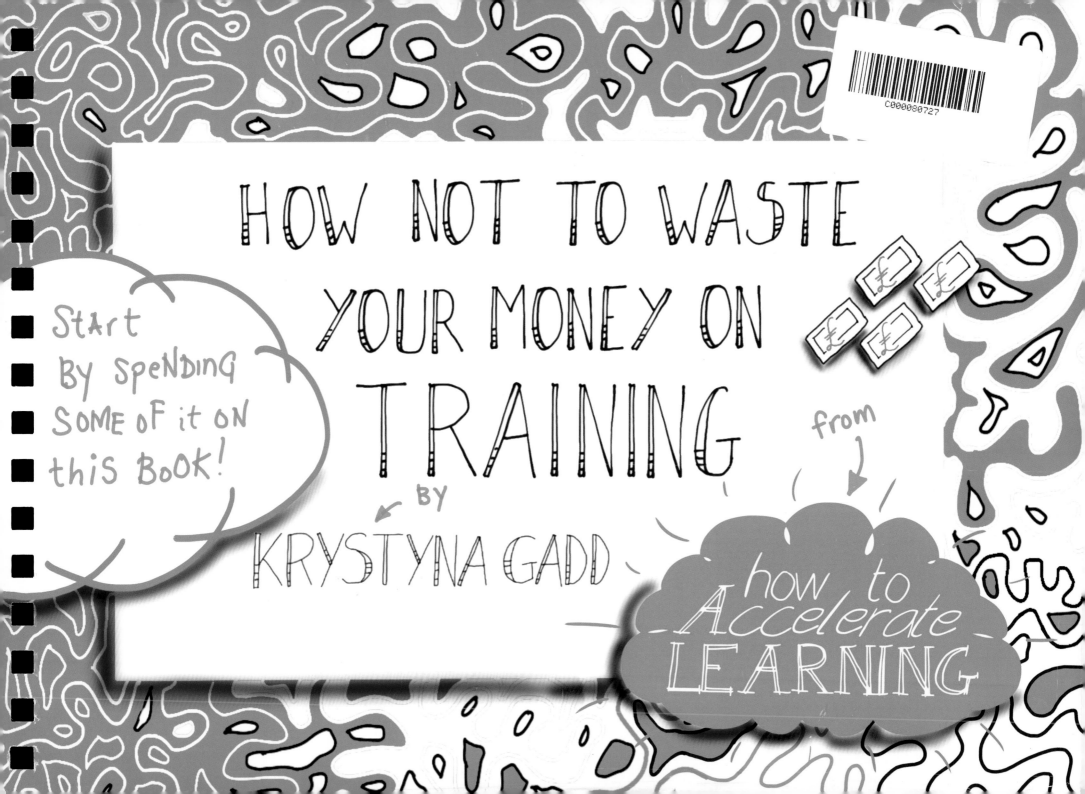

Published by How to Accelerate Learning

The right of the author to be identified as the author of this work has been asserted by her in accordance with the Copyright, Designs and Patents Act 1988.

A catalogue record for this book is available from the British Library

ISBN: 978-1-910848-31-9

Cover design by Krystyna Gadd
Cover layout by Esther Kotecha, EKDesign
Typeset by Avocet Typeset, Somerton, Somerset, TA11 6RT
Printed and bound in the UK

Dedication

I would like to thank Gareth for all your encouragement and support,
not just with the book, but throughout the years in my career.

I thank God for blessing me with a career that I love

Krys
X

Contents

TESTIMONIALS

"If you are serious about cost-effective learning that genuinely drives impact, then this is a book which should interest you!"

Andy Lancaster

Head of Learning and Development Content, CIPD

"Recommended reading for anyone in an L&D function"

Donald H Taylor

Chair, Learning and Performance Institute

"A practical guidebook to help L&Ders navigate their way to becoming a true business partner."

Marie Duncan

Head of L&D, Kibble Education

"This is a valuable resource for those in Learning and Development...and is perhaps even more valuable for those who are not."

John Swallow

Head of L&D Specsavers

"I have no doubt you will find this book a hugely interesting and impactful read."

Karen Grave

President PPMA

please read more!

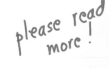

Testimonials

Donald H Taylor
Chair, Learning and Performance Institute
This book is packed with useful advice and insight into when formal learning is the right solution. Drawing on decades of practical experience, it explains clearly, and with practical examples, how to ensure training is deployed only when necessary, and to the greatest effect. Recommended reading for anyone in an L&D function, whether inside an organisation, or supplying services from the outside.

Andy Lancaster,
Head of Learning and Development Content, CIPD.
In a fast-changing world its vital that organisations invest in learning and development not only to stay ahead of the game, but to survive! However, there is never a bottomless pot for investment, often learning budgets are squeezed and senior leaders are increasingly demanding a measurable impact from initiatives. To that end, learning professionals must target learning to meet key organisational needs through effective design and delivery approaches. *How Not To Waste Your Money On Training"* provides valuable insights and tactics on how to maximise learning by aligning it to what the organisation is trying to achieve, simplifying and focussing diagnostic processes, making informed data-driven decisions and effectively presenting solutions. If you are serious about cost-effective learning that genuinely drives impact, then this is a book which should interest you!

Karen Grave
President PPMA (Public Service People Managers Association)
PPMA has been working with Krystyna for only a short time but we have already realised that she is an enormous asset to the field of learning. She has a natural passion and empathy for people, which she combines with creativity and an engineering background to help organisations focus on how best to deliver on training investment. Krystyna's style is deeply engaging, laced with a lot of humour and a willingness to challenge the ridiculous. It's a powerful combination. We love working with her and I have no doubt you will find this book a hugely interesting and impactful read.

Marie Duncan
Head of L&D Kibble Education

Krys is passionate about the unique role Learning & Development can play within organisations and provides a practical guidebook to help L&Ders navigate their way to becoming a true business partner.

I've been an L&D professional for 15 years and wish I'd had this book 15 years ago! It's a brilliant 'back to basics' book about the fundamental, and powerful, role that L&D plays within the organisation. It has taken me outside of my head and helped me refocus on my ultimate purpose and helped me plan as to how I, and the team, can get there.

This is such a practical, real-world and hands-on book that demystifies the current trend of data analytics. It provides useful, everyday tools for using information to prepare and plan for the multiple ways in which L&D can support the business to achieve its goals.

John Swallow
Head of L&D Specsavers

I love Krystyna's new book on how to avoid wasting money on training. It does what is says on the tin. Throughout the book, Krystyna brings her considerable experience of learning and development to the table and focuses on how to get the most bang for your buck. This is a clearly written and easily understandable book which is refreshingly visual. Whatever your level of experience, this book will help you to think through your own challenges from a different perspective. This is a valuable resource for those in Learning and Development...and is perhaps even more valuable for those who are not. If you are going to spend money on training, read this first.

Kevin M. Yates
Fact-Finder for Learning & Development

It made me fall in love with data again! As a Learning & Development practitioner focused on using facts, evidence and data to answer the question, "Did training work?", I applaud the time given in the book for explaining learning analytics. The combination of words, imagery, activities, definitions and exercises for self-reflection support the reader in building actionable knowledge for using data to inform decisions, answer questions and show impact.

Now more than ever, L&D practitioners need skill and capability with using data. The case studies and examples of how to collect, interpret and tell stories with data empowers readers with the knowledge they'll need to be data-literate. It makes data less scary. We don't have to wish or hope L&D is making an impact when there's data to prove it. This book tells that story perfectly!

Colin Steed

Founder of Learning Now TV

Krystyna Gadd's new book is an extremely useful and practical guide for all L&D practitioners who are trying to align their projects to what the business is trying to achieve.

This practically-based work book will help you to collect the right information to inform your decisions on what sort of training is necessary – and more importantly, if training is even required at all to achieve your goals. It is also for you if you want to demonstrate the value of training and need a great way to show it to your business leaders.

Krystyna has the ability to describe often complex issues into easily understood and interesting ways. In particular, I found the Chapter on collecting and analysing business data was expertly described and made a bit of a boring subject (for me) totally absorbing. By the way, this is a must have skill for all future L&D professionals.

The book is interspersed throughout with some very attractive graphics that the author is well-known for and I particularly liked that there are activities to try at the end of each of the chapters to help reinforce what has been covered.

I highly recommend this book and urge all learning and development professionals to read it and keep it close at hand for reference to help you in your learning journey.

Prologue

Do you suspect your budget is going to be wasted on training that isn't really needed? Have you ever wanted to make the process more effective, but been so busy delivering training that you never get the chance to unpack what's working and what's not?

If you answered yes to either of these questions, you're in the right place. That's exactly why I've written *How to Not Waste Your Money on Training*. This book is a practical look at how you can avoid wasting money on training that may not be needed.

Before you invest time in this book, I would love to give you an idea of what you'll get out of it, because your time is important to me. It is about how you can help your colleagues perform better, as well as measuring that improvement.

I have been in the training game for over 30 years. As a trainer-of-trainers for over 10 years, I have observed that trainers and L&D professionals are great at designing and delivering learning experiences, but as a whole, less confident about the analysis and evaluation part of the learning cycle. We tend to be shy about managing stakeholders and aligning with the business too.

As a self-confessed maths geek and former engineer, the learning cycle has always made sense to me:

- Analyse to make sure you know where you're heading
- Design with the end in mind
- Deliver, making sure you are headed in the right direction
- Evaluate to check you have done what you set out to do (closing the loop).

I realise that it also makes sense to a lot of L&D professionals, who may or may not have all the skills, knowledge or confidence to approach learning in a holistic and organisational way.

This book is for you, as an L&D professional, manager or stakeholder in any industry, if you are interested in aligning learning to what your organisation is trying to achieve. It will help you collect the right information to inform your decisions on what sort of learning is most appropriate (if indeed, it is even necessary). It is for you if you'd like to uncover and fulfil your organisation's needs. It is for you also if you have some great ideas on how to do this, but need a little more clarity on how to piece it together. It is for you if you want to demonstrate the value of learning, but need to know how to embark on this journey or continue if you have already begun.

What you'll get from this book:

- A simplified approach to uncovering what an organisation needs
- More clarity on how L&D can perform better by working *with* the organisation
- An approach to ensure tangible outcomes from learning
- Practical tools to help you and the organisation become more agile so that you can achieve your goals

What you'll be able to do:

- Create a plan to successfully understand the organisation and get closer to what it really needs
- Create a plan for managing your stakeholders (and identifying them if you haven't done so yet)
- Analyse the information you collect in a number of different ways
- Present your findings in a number of different ways
- Find the 'story' in your information to inform any decisions
- Make the link between the information you collect and analyse, and the evaluation process

As a seasoned L&D professional, I understand the frustrations of working in environments where L&D is not a priority or does not get the support it needs. I have worked with stakeholders who clearly do not understand the direction of the organisation, let alone the needs of its employees.

Through the book, you may wonder about my reluctance to use training needs analysis or even learning needs analysis. The main reason for this is a shift in my thinking (and hopefully yours too). I believe that not every problem necessarily has a training or learning solution. In any organisation, which in reality is never a closed system, there are many factors as to why something may not be working:

- Lack of resources
- Poor communication

- Poor management
- Faulty systems or processes
- People lacking motivation (not skills or knowledge)
- Lack of clear goals and targets
- People not empowered to make the changes required
- Silo-working where mistakes are repeated and not shared
- Lack of a shared vision
- Trust issues

This is to name just a few. Each organisation will have its own barriers to growth, unique to itself and its culture. Having said that, there are many common barriers that can be seen across the board in many sectors.

What has been interesting in the last few years is the development of The New Learning Organisation[1] through research by Towards Maturity. In their report in May 2017, they shared disappointment of Peter Senge's vision of the Learning Organisation[2] not even being close to happening. Senge shared his vision on how organisations could problem-solve using systems-thinking and hence become 'learning organisations'. Towards Maturity also shared their new vision, underpinned not just by desire or hope, but by research and focus on the top deck*, to guide our thinking on The New Learning Organisation.

*The top deck are those organisations identified through this research as already being high performing.

Below is a visual summarising what that will look like. As you will see, at the heart of The New Learning Organisation is **Clarity of Purpose**. Perhaps, like me, you find this unsurprising. After all, clarity of purpose is key to improving performance. It goes hand-in-hand with intelligent decision-making, which also features in any new learning organisation. If this is so, it naturally follows that in L&D we should be practising this by:

- Infiltrating* the organisation to be clear about its purpose
- Determining which key metrics help us to further clarify how close we are to meeting the goals

*Infiltrating the organisation, ninja-like and getting under its skin to understand what it needs and how it works, as well as how it does not!

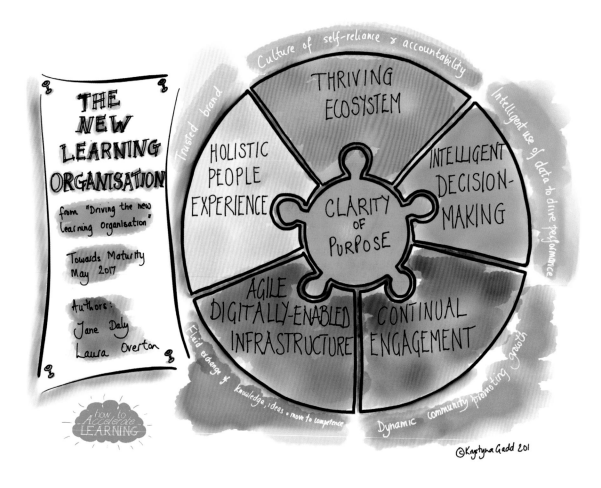

To have a **Thriving Ecosystem**, where there is a culture of self-reliance and accountability, L&D needs to be informed through digging deeper into what the organisation needs to learn, how and when. With the right information, L&D can help create an **Agile and Digitally Enabled Infrastructure**, rich in relevant learning experiences in a variety of different formats. This will include onboarding to create that **Holistic People Experience**. All of these, when working together, consistently create a trusted company brand where people thrive and grow. When people thrive and innovation in learning is the norm, the top deck is three times more likely to report that "learning innovation has resulted in an impact on business innovation and on staff motivation".[1]

Another perspective is that of Performance Consulting[4] where L&D adopt an approach to align with the organisation. Any learning content will also be aligned to strategic goals and there will be an obvious link to performance.

This book hopes to address a key piece of the jigsaw that is missing – that we can only have clarity and make informed decisions if we *really know* what is going on in the organisations we work with and in. This means not just having *one* person's viewpoint, but as clear a picture as possible. To do this, we need to venture into a world of questions, curiosity and finding meaning in information.

Once you begin on this journey and discover how it will help build a picture of the organisations you work for, there will be no going back.

I have set the scene of where L&D needs to head. *How to Not Waste Your Money on Training* is going to help you go there. The New Learning Organisation model created by Towards Maturity gives us a destination, but this book will take you on the journey.

In Chapter 1, you will explore how you in L&D can get more closely aligned to what the organisation really needs as well as considering different consultancy models to follow. A key part to alignment will be identifying and managing your stakeholders and you will be given a simple tool to achieve this.

In Chapter 2, you will be led gently to consider whether an in-depth analysis is always needed and also whether the analysis can always be planned. You may feel daunted by the prospect of any analysis, let alone deciding the level required. Rest assured that you can skip the analysis part completely at times, if you feel in line with what the organisation needs and have your finger on the pulse.

Understanding the level of analysis will be key and there will be some simple ways in which you can identify the level. By the end, you should be able to put together a plan for your learning needs analysis, including the methods and resources you will need.

Chapter 3 is where you will look at what data to collect and how to ensure you keep an eye on what the organisation is trying to achieve. We will keep it simple here and make sure the link between learning and performance is at the forefront of our minds. If you feel nervous about this part, then what you have learned in Chapter 1 will really help. Those relationships you have fostered with key stakeholders will stand you in good stead to decide, in partnership, what needs to be measured and more importantly who will measure it. It is not always L&D's role to measure performance improvements, so those partnerships will be key.

The final piece of the puzzle will be in presenting the data in a format that makes sense to those interested in the results of your LNA. Chapter 4 looks at how different types of graphs can uncover the story that is behind what is happening in the organisation. Again, simplicity will be key. You will learn (if you don't already know) how to set great objectives and outcomes for any learning you have planned. Bloom's Taxonomy is a great model for helping you create objectives that are focussed and specific as well as measurable.

How to read this book:

This is not just a textbook to gather dust on a shelf. It has some text to inform you, but it is essentially a workbook to work through. It has practical exercises that will lead you through each objective set out at the start of every chapter. You may have already done some of what I will suggest. Hence, feel free to skip those skills that you feel you have already mastered.

I would suggest skim-reading the whole book so that you get an overall picture of the process from start to finish. Then, to make the most of your time, work through the text and the case study as well as the activities in sequence.

Chapter 1 does not need a specific project to work on as it focusses on being able to position your role in L&D within the organisation. In subsequent chapters, it will be useful for you to have a specific learning need defined so that you can use it to do your analysis.

Take a break between working through each chapter to reflect on what you have done and what you will refine next time you need to use the process. Not every project will require the same level of work. Some steps may seem easier on different projects.

There is a case study that runs like a thread through the book and you will see this when you see this image:

Let's get to it!

Who to know and how to reach them

Objectives:

By the end of this chapter you will be able to:

1.1   Through your action planning sheet, describe how you in L&D can get more closely aligned with (infiltrate) the business.
1.2   Consider which consultancy model to use in stakeholder engagement to determine the brief.
1.3   Identify your stakeholders and classify them according to their impact and support.

"Begin with the end in mind." – **Stephen Covey**

*"Context is everything – you cannot design anything in a vacuum." – **Krystyna Gadd***

Aligning with the business

A long time ago, more years than I care to remember, I was a chemical engineer and fuel technologist. As an engineer, I would never have considered embarking on a project without knowing exactly what was going to come out the other end and how we would know it was a success. Whether it was designing a device for transporting micro fine coal or collecting data to assess the suitability of a site for a wind farm, it all needed a crystal-clear vision for what the outcomes would be.

My approach to L&D has been pretty much the same: determine what is needed, design something to meet those needs, then find out if you have met those needs.

Since moving into the L&D world, I have been at times surprised how readily people will embark on a project without really knowing how it will pan out. The following is a scenario that is all too familiar...

On social media, an L&D professional reached out to peers for ideas on some activities for conflict management. Nothing unusual in that, you might think. This professional shared also that they were running a leadership event and the week before that event, one of the senior team had suggested that "adding something on conflict management would be useful".

Trying to shoehorn in something at this late stage of the game can be incredibly stressful and also difficult. Panic can set in and decisions on what to include what to take out can be made in haste. I don't suppose you've encountered this sort of scenario where L&D has been roped into providing training without even pausing for breath?

Before jumping in and providing the requested training, I suggested asking the following questions:

- What is happening now that makes you think it is a problem?
- How will learning about conflict management help?
- How will you know it has helped?

I made a further suggestion: dig deeper to find your focus, so you know that when you are shoehorning this in at the last minute, it will have some impact and not detract from what has already been planned.

Setting off without a crystal-clear idea of what the outputs and outcomes will be is a little like this...

Imagine you are a high-class perfumer and a potential client asks you to create a lovely new fragrance. Immediately, you think of some key ingredients: oil of bergamot, jasmine and maybe musk. You design a beautiful bottle, the like of which has never been seen before,

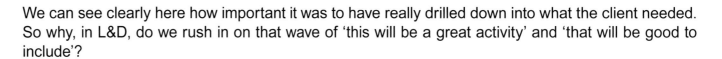

and packaging to die for. You create your fragrance, present it to the client, who says, "It's lovely but I was after a nice smell for a new air freshener we are designing."

We can see clearly here how important it was to have really drilled down into what the client needed. So why, in L&D, do we rush in on that wave of 'this will be a great activity' and 'that will be good to include'?

I am not saying we never look into the detail of what outputs we want to achieve, but I hear so many stories of how L&D doesn't have time to drill down into what stakeholders need, how you are not given time, resources or people. So, is this what really stops us?

It can be a number of different things that stop us from getting to the real needs right up front:

- Lack of money
- Lack of time
- Lack of resources
- Stakeholders don't really know what they want
- We don't know the right questions to ask

Let's imagine that you already understand the business deeply. When you get a myriad of requests from every department, your depth of knowledge means you can prioritise those requests, knowing what the business *really* needs at any given time. It also means you can, if people are insistent on doing something *right now*, make a strong business case to get adequate resources to complete the work when it is needed.

ACTIVITY

Objective 1.1

From research completed by Towards Maturity[1], the top deck is 50% more likely to say that their work (in L&D) is linked to the organisation's performance (84% agree). They are also more likely to agree that learning is aligned with the business plan (97% agree).

This makes a strong case for everyone to begin aligning L&D to the organisation's plan. Using the action planning sheet, make notes* on what you might choose to do to get more closely aligned to the business. Here are some suggestions:

1. Read through the corporate/business plans for your whole organisation and make notes on the big picture: the purpose of the organisation
2. Look at your organisation's website. Can you determine its purpose from there? Do your customers know what you are about?
3. Have you any specific goals for this year in your team?
4. Are there new areas of business you are looking into?
5. Ask your CEO where the business needs to most improve performance to have the biggest impact. (Ask others too and see if they agree!)
6. Attend meetings all over the business – volunteer to make tea, notes or just be nosey. Ask questions if you do not understand something and note down* what happened and what the outputs or issues raised were.

*By making notes, you may start to make connections in your brain about what might be going wrong (or right) in the organisation. It also means that you can refer to the meetings you attended when you raise it as an issue.

Let's imagine there's a performance issue with a team. The line manager has some ideas about what is causing the issue but comes to L&D to dig deeper. L&D looks at the line manager's perspective and suggests considering what the team thinks might be causing the issue, as well as approaching some of their customers. Budgets and resources approved, you quickly spring into action gathering customer feedback and getting the team together for an hour without their line manager.

You approach the whole scenario with curiosity, not blame and uncover:

- A glitch in the process of dealing with customer complaints
- Some personality clashes in the team
- Unrealistic expectations of performance

What in the past may have been dealt with in a one-day workshop for the whole team might be solved with no classroom time at all. It is not always easy to deal with these issues, but at least you are not masking them, hoping for the best that a training course will solve the problem.

The whole purpose of L&D is not to design and deliver learning, but to help the business improve its performance. In his book *Employee Training and Developmen*[4], Raymond Noe shares a very simple diagram of the role of training (and hence, you might say, L&D too). I have redrawn this diagram below:

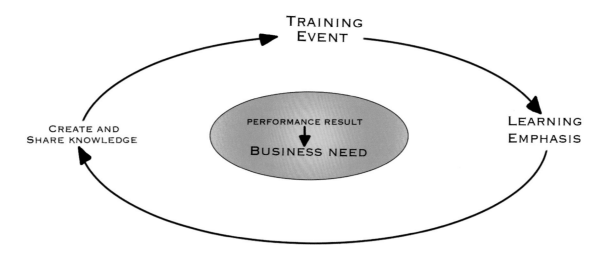

Here, there is a clear link between an individual on the job achieving a performance result and satisfying a need within the business. At times, it may be through identifying performance gaps that can be filled with learning. At other times, it may be that you have done a little digging and found something other than a lack of knowledge or skill to be the cause of a performance issue. It is important to know the difference.

"The three critical areas that bridge the gap between learning events and on-the-job performance are: improving needs analysis; building learner motivation; enabling manager support."[5]

If we can make substantial improvements in these three areas then, maybe we can move some way towards demonstrating a measurable link with learning and performance.

Kevin M. Yates an advocate and practitioner in the performance approach to delivering learning asks three questions before embarking on any training[19]:

1. What's happening in the organisation?
2. What is the organisations goal?
3. What performance requirements are needed to achieve your organisations goal?

Kevin calls himself a 'Fact-finder' is the Learning and Technology Manager for McDonalds in the US.

At this point in time, you may be at the beginning of your curious journey. If it is not in your nature to be nosey, then begin by just asking 'why?' and keep asking until you get to the root of an issue. In fact, just by asking five 'whys'[7] in succession, you'll often get a clear picture.

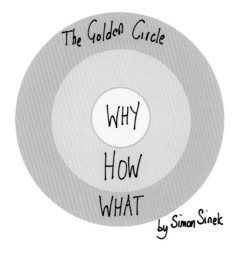

The Golden Circle

WHY

HOW

WHAT

by Simon Sinek

Simon Sinek, in his book *Start With Why*[7], talks about the Golden Circle. Lots of organisations know 'what' they do and 'how' they do it, but not so many know 'why'. When you find out the real 'why', issues become much clearer and you can work towards a goal with purpose.

A good number of organisations I interact with will describe their L&D function as 'reactive' rather than 'proactive', meaning that when a stakeholder asks them to do something, they respond in as helpful a way as possible, perhaps launching into solution-mode a little too quickly.

What could be wrong with that? you might wonder. Let's unpack this with an easy example.

Customer engagement scores are down and the Head of Customer Service asks you to run some refresher training, rolling it out to all the staff, starting in four weeks' time and for a period of six weeks to make sure all staff manage to participate. Scores are measured before and after to determine the effectiveness, knowing that better engagement scores lead to longer and more profitable customer relationships.

This could go two ways:

1. Scores are improved and justify the expenditure because of the link with profitability. Nothing needs to change and L&D carries on as before.
2. Scores do not improve and the Head of Customer Service asks L&D what went wrong.

In the second scenario, there could be a lot of soul-searching by L&D (and finger-pointing by others). What were the evaluation sheets like? The participants seemed to enjoy the training and scored the course quite highly. There are so many questions I know you might be asking:

- Was the original brief correct?
- What evidence was there to support the brief was or was not correct?
- Is there something else unknown that was the real cause of the problem?
- Is anyone else in the market experiencing the same issues?
- Are our products in line with competitors'?
- Were the right people targeted in the right way?
- Were the best topics covered?
- Was there enough skills practice?
- Did the line managers follow up after the training?
- Is there a hotspot for the low scores? If yes, can you identify areas or teams?

Just looking at these questions, you may ask why these were not asked *before* the training was delivered. And you'd be right. It can be more difficult to unpick this after the event.

Let's make some changes to the original example so we can compare. Imagine you asked the questions above when the Head of Customer Service asks you to roll out the training. Here's what you might say:

"Could I just have 10 minutes of your time to ask some questions about this, so we can be absolutely sure we are delivering the right thing?"

I would be surprised if any Head of Customer Service worth their salt would not pause just for a second and say 'yes', glad of the offer to further investigate the underlying causes.

L&D needs to find out every 'why' before embarking on any learning delivery, especially training. You can do that by infiltrating the organisation like this:

- Reading organisational plans
- Familiarising yourself with the mission, vision, values and corporate goals
- Going to meetings to make notes (or even tea!), listening and observing

- Discussing with other L&D team members
- Having an in-depth conversation with the *right* stakeholders about uncovering needs, not just learning or training needs

If you start with this list and take action, you will get under the skin of the organisation. You will 'infiltrate' it. You will get a better, deeper understanding of what it is trying to achieve and what might get in its way.

A more consultative approach

The simple act of asking this one question – *can we talk to be sure we're delivering the right thing?* – can have a profound effect on the way you begin to operate with or within an organisation. Regardless of whether you are an external consultant or an internal L&D professional, this one question will give your stakeholder (or stakeholders) an opportunity to pause to consider what is really going on and be heard. It can be the first step to establishing trust in a relationship, old or new, as well as redefining the way in which you work together to find the right solutions for the organisation. This can be the start of a new more consultative approach to learning and development.

People speak about using a consultancy approach, but what does that mean in practice? In her article *Treating Learning Content as a Strategic Business Asset*, Kelly Rider, vice president of SAP learning organisation, and responsible for setting the learning content strategy and experience for over 80,000 people, writes about learning content being aligned to strategic business goals. My take? It goes even deeper than this. Here's how...

When we adopt a true consultancy approach, learning is not the only item on our agenda. We ask questions that go beyond learning, the purpose of which is to uncover the true nature of the problems the organisation faces. One day, I hope we will move away from an accusation levelled at us in L&D that "it is rare for learning to align with the business at inception."[3]

This might seem daunting to an individual who has not had the breadth of experience to understand all that may happen in a business; digging deeper to uncover business deficiencies may serve to uncover their own lack of knowledge and skills. Let me reassure you here. If that does apply to you, just because you have uncovered something that does not quite work in an organisation does not mean you have to know how to solve it. That is the beauty of consulting in partnership with the stakeholders. If you happen to stumble upon something that may be an issue, previously unseen, the stakeholders may have a solution or number of solutions. Yours is not the responsibility to solve a problem alone, but to identify there is an issue.

Raymond Noe, Professor of Management at the Ohio State University and author of the book *Employee Training and Development*, supports this by saying, "To fully serve the organisation, L&D professionals must first understand it. This need to understand the organisation requires us to operate outside the confines of the L&D department or team and involve ourselves in the wider context of the whole organisation."[4]

So, consider what your role might be in the consultancy process:

- Asking questions and being curious
- Being brave enough to ask the 'daft question'
- Identifying those who will be key in defining the problem
- Identifying those who will be key in agreeing the right solution and able to measure its success
- Understanding more deeply how the business operates and where there might be a disconnect.

Case Study Part 1

I was once called into a client to deliver a suite of training topics to a group of team leaders. Flattering though it was to be asked and given this on a plate, it got my curiosity going and questions bubbled up in my mind:

- Why this group of people?
- Why now?
- Why these subjects?
- What has been happening?
- What has not been happening?

The answer to the first question from the managing director (MD) was "because the senior team have had some training, we thought it would be nice for the team leaders to have some too". The word 'nice' alerted me to a load more questions:

- How will you measure if it has been a success?
- What if nothing changes in six months? Who will you blame?
- What makes you think they need any training?
- Is there something else happening, other than a lack of skills or knowledge?

It may be obvious that the MD would blame me, so my response was to ask more questions. After two hours, he finally said, "I think we need you to do a needs analysis, Krys". Music to my ears! I put together a proposal of how long it might take and what my approach would be. This was approved and I began a journey with this client, which would uncover not only what training was needed, but also some issues that had nothing to do with training.

Learning and development professionals are often in a unique position of being able to see many perspectives. The finance team gets to see the finance perspective and maybe how purchasing interacts. Sales gets to see the sales perspective and maybe how marketing operates. In L&D, though, we span the whole organisation, able to join dots and make connections like no other function. Make the most of it! Learn not only what the organisation does but how. Learn which interactions work and which don't. Dig deep into the purpose of what the organisation is trying to do (keeping Simon Sinek's 'why' idea front-of-mind).

To further adopt that consultancy approach, you need to have strategies on how to cope in moments when you are caught off-guard, maybe in the corridor, and asked to deliver a training programme. In those moments, you need to have some delaying tactics... Do not agree to anything in haste!

The HIRE model is a simple tool drawn from a number of models concerned with questioning, used in coaching mainly. I have found it to be invaluable in giving me that time to ask meaningful questions, while delaying the rush to thinking a training solution is the way to go.

Another approach could be to use Cathy Moore's action-mapping approach[8]. Cathy Moore is an internationally recognised training designer and published author in this field. Her action-mapping approach can help to define what to get out of training, once you have determined that training is the actual solution. I prefer to keep an open mind throughout the whole process, not assuming that when someone comes to me to ask for training that training is actually what they truly need.

A third approach is to use the Performance Consultancy approach[9] by Nigel Harrison, chartered business psychologist, where the approach is to become a business partner, rather than an 'order taker'.

ACTIVITY

Objective 1.2

Look through the summaries of the three consultancy approaches and make some notes. Do some more research on each to see which one will suit your organisation and your L&D team.

The three approaches are:

    1.2.1   HIRE

    1.2.2   Action-planning

    1.2.3   Performance consulting

Managing your stakeholders

In 2009, Rosemary Harrison[20], fellow of the CIPD and a leading academic and author in L&D, said, "Strategic business partnerships between L&D professionals and senior managers may still be relatively rare but strategically focussed partnerships at middle management level are increasingly expected". Have things moved on? Of the top deck identified by Towards Maturity[10], 91% of L&D say business leaders recognise that their learning interventions are aligned with the overall business plan. Sadly, the top deck is a small minority of all the businesses out there and we cannot assume this practice is as widely spread as this sample indicates.

Earlier, I mentioned working with the *right* stakeholders. That may be a real sticking point to say the least! How do you find out who are the right stakeholders to work with? I like using the Stakeholder Analysis Grid. It is best to do this in conjunction with other people, if you are in an internal team, or ask your client to do this with their team for you, if you are an external consultant.

Let's explore what the Stakeholder Analysis Grid (derived from Mendelow's Power-Interest Grid[11]) is about. This is the one I use in my work and have found most applicable to the context of L&D.

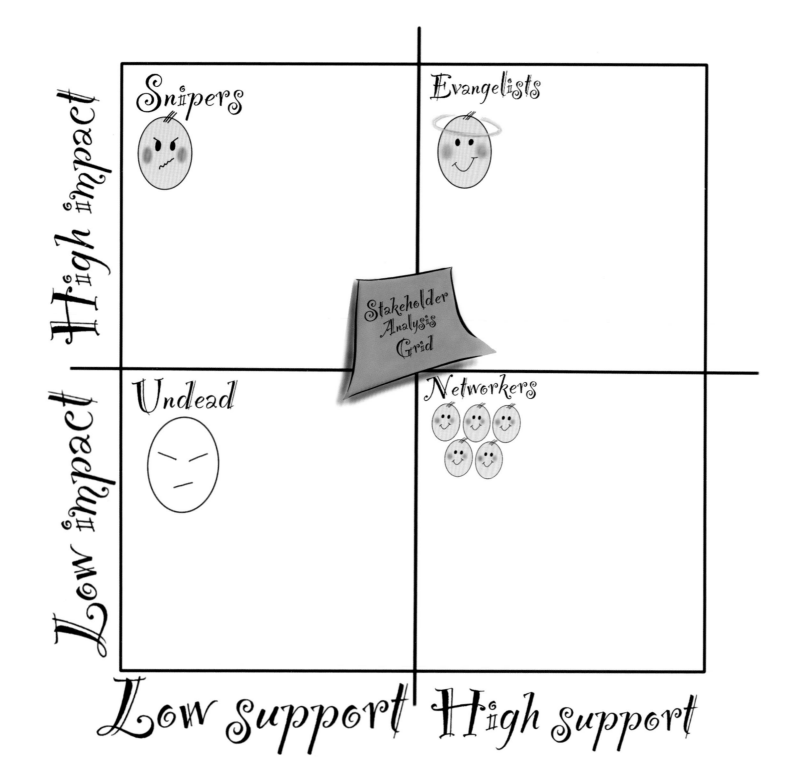

In brief, you can categorise your stakeholders according to the grid above:

- **Undead** (low support and low impact) – not of much use – spend as little time as possible with this group.
- **Snipers** (low support but high impact) – if you can win these over, they will become the evangelists who will not only support you, but will get things done for you – win them over by demonstrating the value you bring and speaking to them on their terms about what you can do for them.
- **Networkers** (high support but low impact) – boost morale when you need it but have little influence to get things moving in the organisation – keep them on board and watch out, because they may grow in their influence!
- **Evangelists** (high support and high impact) – boost morale as well as being a mover and shaker in the organisation – spend most of your time on these and keep them sweet – use them to exert influence where you cannot.

ACTIVITY

Objective 1.3

Use this grid to identify your own stakeholders and perform an analysis on them. If you are doing this as a group exercise, use a flipchart or stick masking tape on the floor or wall in a grid, using Post-its to place names of the stakeholders.

As a group exercise, I would suggest the following:

1. Gather those people in your team who will be able to identify the stakeholders that impact and influence your work in L&D.
2. Explain the stakeholder analysis grid or alternatively watch this short video: https://youtu.be/k8Hb0mcFmNo.
3. Give everyone some Post-its and pens.
4. Using one Post-it per named person, ask them to name your stakeholders and place them where they think they are on the grid. Do this without discussion and ask people not to be influenced by others' placement of stakeholders. You will get an opportunity to discuss once all the stakeholders have been identified and placed.
5. Start with the Undead and agree which ones fall into this category. There may be some discussion as to whether they are

really Undead or Snipers, so be willing to be flexible and move them into the appropriate box.

6. Now discuss the Networkers and agree those people that are supportive, but may not have any impact in the organisation. Some shifting of Post-its may happen here too.

7. Move now onto the Evangelists and the Snipers. Allow people time to have a look who has been placed where. There may be discussions that arise about who should be where. There may be strong opinions on this. Allow the discussion to evolve. Maybe some people's Evangelists are other people's Snipers. Make notes on how they think you might convert the Snipers in this category into Evangelists.

8. Do not move Snipers from where they are; instead have an action plan of how to convert the Snipers.

In the chapter summary below, you will see how completing these activities will get you ready for the next step.

Coming up in the next chapter, we'll look at the needs of the business. Now, not all projects will require a thorough needs analysis, but remember to not dismiss out of hand the benefits of stopping, pausing and questioning any request for training that may come to your team.

As I've mentioned, in some cases, a conversation with a stakeholder may be sufficient, where you've correctly identified a need. There may be times when it will not be sufficient, such as when:

- There are several stakeholders involved, each with a very different requirement
- The outcomes from the learning intervention (or training) will have a profound effect on how the organisation runs for many years (management development, innovation initiatives, change management)
- The outcomes are unclear and yet you are required to demonstrate the value you will bring to the organisation
- Something does not seem to add up in your estimation and maybe there are rumours of the causes.

Let's look now at what stakeholders need and where to go from there.

Just a quick recap of what you have covered in this chapter and what you should be able to do:

Objectives:

1.1 Though your action planning sheet, describe how you in L&D can get more closely aligned with (infiltrate) the business – by completing activity 1.

Completed (date and sign)...

1.2 Choose a consultancy model to use in stakeholder engagement to determine the brief – by completing activity 2.

Completed (date and sign)...

1.3 Identify your stakeholders and classify them according to their impact and support – by completing activity 3.

Completed (date and sign)...

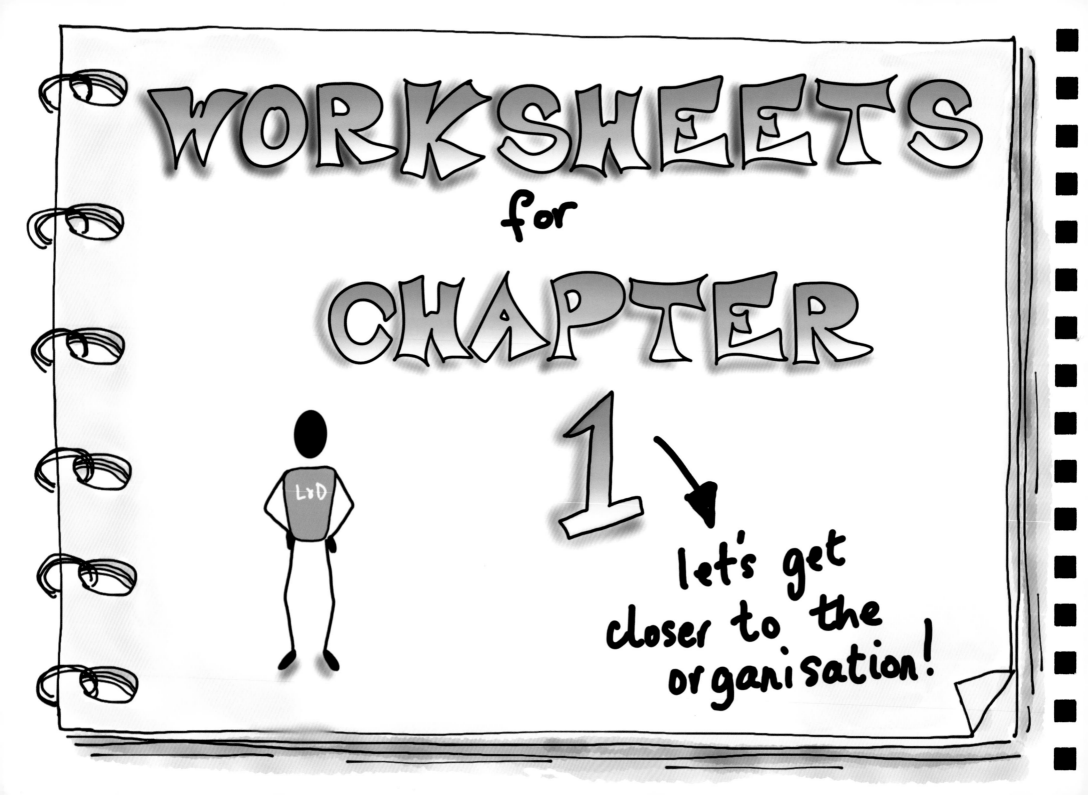

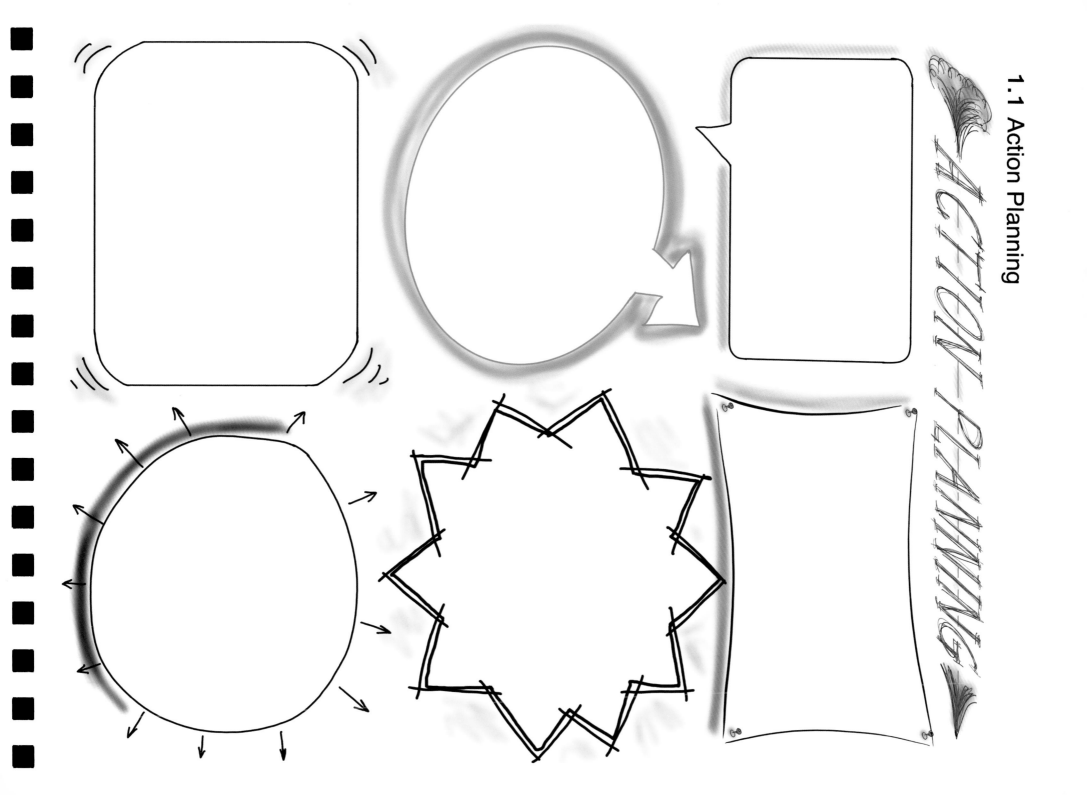

1.2.1 Great Questions to Uncover Needs

When dealing with your stakeholders it is important to ask the right questions, so that you can really uncover the needs that the training is meant to meet. In a conversation with a stakeholder or client, a good model to use is the **HIRE** model. This has been devised by Krystyna Gadd and drawn from several coaching and consultancy approaches.

List questions for each phase in the boxes provided below:

H	Tell me what is **HAPPENING**?
I	What are the underlying **ISSUES**?
R	What are the **RAMIFICATIONS** of these problems?
E	What do you **EXPECT**? (the benefits)

H	Tell me about what is happening just now? Tell me about what is not happening just now? Why now? Who is(not) involved? Who should be involved? How long has this been going on? Who are the key people? What have you tried?
I	What are the underlying issues? What might have triggered this/these? What has gone well? How did it happen? Why did it happen? What would you do to prevent this in the future? What changes might have triggered this? Have you any evidence?
R	What are the ramifications of not addressing these problems? If you solve this what will you achieve? If you do not solve this what will happen? What is the worst that can happen? What is the cost of not doing this? What is the cost of doing this? How is this impacting the stakeholders? What are the implications to the wider organisation? How do people feel about this?

E	What do you expect to get from this? What are your priorities? What will really make a difference? Where do you want to be in 6 months? What does "good" look like? What is the budget? What are the constraints? Is there anything else that we have not thought of?

ACTION MAPPING

Design any type of training

Live – elearning – on demand – spaced over time – in the workflow

Start with the performance problem, not the content.

1 What change do we want to see in business performance?
A measure we already use will increase/decrease number%
by date as people in a specific group DO something.

2 What do people need to DO on the job to reach our goal?
- ✗ know, understand, define, be aware...
- ✓ greet the customer, enter the data, persuade the team, reject the bribe, polish the widget...

Why aren't they doing it? Will training help?

WILL TRAINING HELP?

3 When the flowchart says training is part of the solution...
How can we help people PRACTICE what they need to do?

Show, don't tell

THEY MAKE A DECISION → THEY SEE THE CONSEQUENCE

Give them realistic challenges and let them pull the information they need.

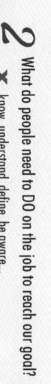

4 What's the MINIMUM information that people need to complete the practice activity? What's the best way to provide it?

blah blah blah quiz

JOB AID or MEMORY?

Consider spacing the activities over time. A one-time course or event is rarely the best solution.

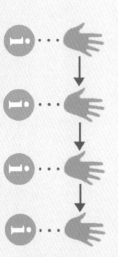

They just need info for this task, not training

Don't include "nice to know"

Everything in the map supports the goal.

LEARN MORE AT CATHY-MOORE.COM

1 The contract
- The problem
- Expected outcome
- How Long?

2 Who is involved?

3 What are they doing now?

Current state

4 What do you want them to do?

Desired state

5 What is the value of the gap?

What is the cost of doing nothing?

£

6 Causes
- Knowledge
- Skill
- Motivation
- Environment

Potential solutions

List all possible ideas

Prioritised solutions

7 Action plan
- Who
- What
- When

Was the contract met?

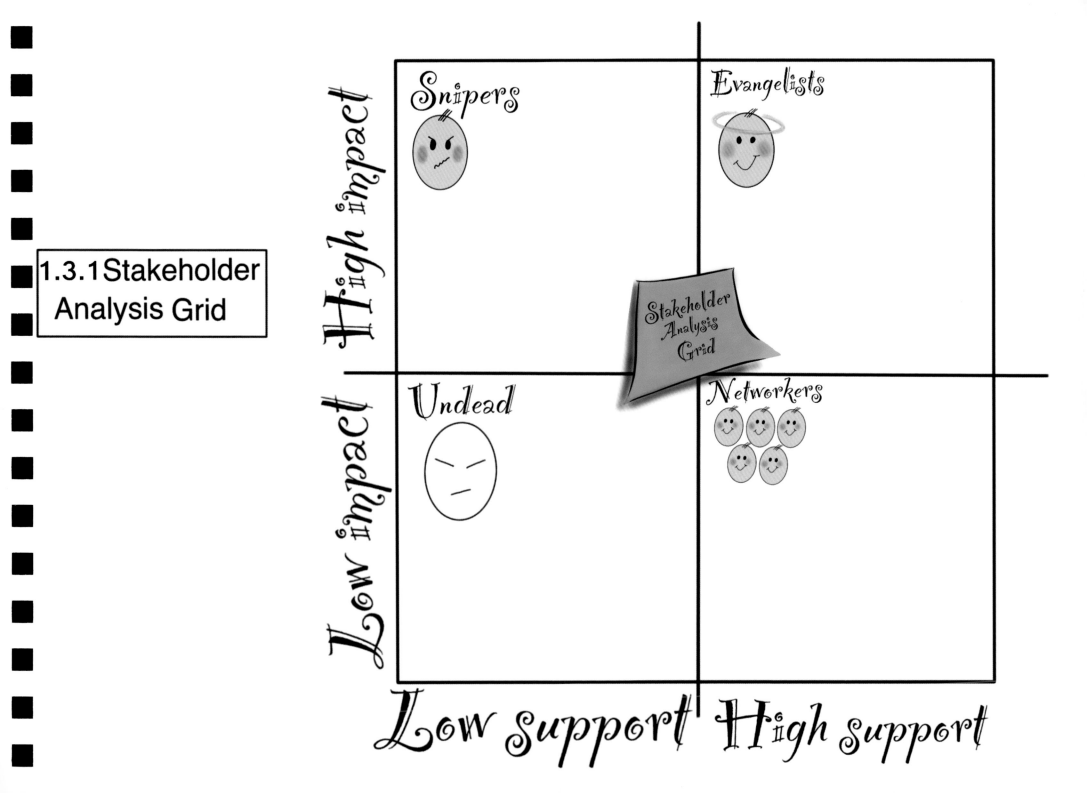

1.3.1 Stakeholder Analysis Grid

Definition of stakeholder:
- a person with an interest or concern in something, especially in business
- anyone who has an interest in what you do as an individual or a team and can support you as well as provide some influence in the organisation

	Stakeholder name	Title	Interested in….	Supportive?	Impact in the organisation?
1	Martin Smith	Customer Services Manager	Customer feedback Number of customer complaints	4/10	9/10
1					
2					
3					
4					
5					

1.3.2 Stakeholder Identification and Analysis

By identifying your stakeholders, it makes it clear to you and the people whose needs you wish to identify, which people you need to consult when assessing needs. These are the people who when everything is going well, will be pleased with what you are doing (and may even tell you!) They are also those people who when things are not going so well, they will be grumbling and making it known that they are not happy.

The key to managing a number of stakeholders is to understand which ones to spend most time with because:
- They are supportive of you and your team
- They have impact in the organisation and can make things happen when you need them to

Having identified your key stakeholders, the next step is to do an analysis of them using the stakeholder analysis grid.

Place the number of your stakeholder on the grid. X marks the spot where I think Martin Smith, the Customer Services Manager lies. He falls into the category of "sniper", but with a little effort could become an evangelist.

Now you need to plan what you will do with them and how much time to spend with them

		Priority	Stakeholder name	Interested in….	Useful for……	Actions
1	E					
2	E					
3	E					

4	S				
5	S				
6	N				
7	N				

E = Evangelists
N = Networkers
S = Snipers
U = Undead

Name	
Position	
Company	
Date	
Notes	

Step 1 – What's going on?	What needs changing?	
This bit is about really finding out what the pain is – what isn't going the way we want/need it to…	What are the irritations that are driving you to action?	
This bit is about really finding out who is involved often it's more that we first think:	Who's involved?	
	Who are the stakeholders?	
	Who is affected by the problem?	
	Who might influence the situation?	
	What information do we have about the problem?	
	What do we know about the causes?	
	What else might we need to know?	

Step 2 – What's success	What is your vision of an ideal future?	
This bit is about imagining how things could be – if you could wave a magic wand…	How will it be different? When the issue is resolved what will you see, hear, feel? What outcome do you want? What must be achieved? What must not happen? What do your stakeholders want? What resources are you willing to invest?	

How to figure out what they need

Objectives:

By the end of the chapter, you will be able to:

2.1 Describe situations where an in-depth analysis is or is not required.
2.2 Differentiate between a planned and unplanned needs analysis.
2.3 Categorise correctly the level of needs analysis to undertake.
2.4 List some appropriate methods for analysing needs for groups and individuals.
2.5 With the use of notes, choose a triangulation approach to needs analysis by selecting three methods for some given case studies.
2.6 Put together a plan for conducting an analysis, including time and resources required.

"Would you tell me, please, which way I ought to go from here?"
"That depends a good deal on where you want to get to."
"I don't much care where –"
"Then it doesn't matter which way you go."

- Lewis Carroll, Alice in Wonderland

In Chapter 1, we looked at the overall context of learning within the organisation, infiltrating it to find the right people and problems, and managing and categorising stakeholders. If you have completed the activities, you will have a better idea of what the organisation is trying to achieve, who you need to work with and also who might be measuring the success of any interventions you design. 'Interventions' could mean any one of over 100 different ways to learn. See Appendix C for more details.

What we are trying to achieve in L&D is a partnership where you support line managers to develop teams to the best of their ability. According to Raymond Noe[4], the role of employees and managers is to:

- *Manage individual performance* – motivate employees to change performance, provide performance feedback and monitor training activities.
- *Develop employees* – explain work assignments and provide technical expertise, amongst other things.

You assist them where needed and leave them when they can manage things by themselves. This last sentence may seem a little scary – what if line managers don't need L&D to develop their teams anymore? We could get into a whole debate on this one! As line managers, their interests will always lie in getting the job done better, not always through learning. In L&D, our interests will always be in learning how to learn better, keeping up to date with the latest trends in learning. As such, I believe there will always be a support role there for L&D.

Do you need to dig deeper?

As mentioned at the end of Chapter 1, a stakeholder conversation may be all that is needed to determine which, *if any*, learning intervention is required. This might be the case when you have already infiltrated the organisation, understood its main goals and purpose. It may also be the case that it 'feels right' because the stakeholder has correctly identified the performance issue or lack of success that needs to be rectified.

A great example might be where a line manager has noticed an increase in customer complaints and has already identified that it stems from a lack of knowledge on a specific product or process. They have checked in with the team and shown that both they and their customers agree on the underlying issue. If the relationship with that line manager is established and no alarm bells are ringing after your conversation (using that consultative approach, of course), it is often safe to go ahead and agree performance objectives, learning outcomes and measures. Following on from that agreement, you can go ahead with the design.

If you feel there is something wrong with the story you are hearing and something does not quite feel right, then do not ignore those feelings. Whenever I have done so, I learnt to my cost that I should have listened to my gut instinct.

ACTIVITY

Objective 2.1

If you are in any doubt about whether you should go ahead with some training/learning, then use our quick checklist to reassure yourself.

An example springs to mind from a few years ago. I was driving along the M62 leaving a workshop, when I received a desperate phone call from a colleague. They were meant to be delivering two half-day sessions (one week apart) on presentation skills but had not managed to 'pull something together'. This was alarm bell number one to me. The first half-day was in three days' time. 'With me being such an expert', they said they were sure I could pull something from what I already had. Alarm bell number two!

I asked some questions (obviously the place to start!):

- Who were the attendees?
- Why did they need to learn how to present?
- How would they benefit from this?

What I did not ask was:

- Have they requested this training?
- What experience did they have in presenting?
- How did these experiences pan out?
- At this point in their career, what was their greatest need?

The answers to the questions I did ask were sketchy to say the least, but my alarm bells were not ringing loud enough due to being tired and driving. Lesson learned! Make time to gather your thoughts and pose the right questions when you can give it your full attention.

You may be wondering what happened as a result of not getting the information. I ran the sessions, of course! In the first half-day session, there were 20 people there and the vibes from the session were high. People seemed to engage in the activities and responses were good. Day two? Only 7 out of the 20 turned up to the half-day session, much to my disappointment. Moreover, it seemed to be those people who were already good at presenting. The ones who seemed to need it most were a no-show.

What I learned after some reflection was this:

- The attendees were never asked if presentation skills training was something they really needed.
- Those who were really nervous presenters were freaked out by having to present to those who were confident.
- The actual needs of the attendees were never really investigated. The two half-day sessions were part of an induction week and the rest of the week was similar.
- In previous years, feedback on the sessions had been good but there were never any measures of how useful or effective the training had been in the attendees' roles.
- I would never do someone a favour in this way again! (I made myself a promise.) In the end, all it would do was tarnish my reputation.

Seeing beyond the orange juice

It is easy to get swept along with urgent needs when, if you spent a little more time digging, you would see them for what they are: *wants*.

Imagine a scenario where someone comes to you and says that they want a glass of orange juice. After a little investigating and questioning, you discover that they actually need their thirst quenching. Having discovered the real need, you can then prescribe many alternate solutions:

- A glass of water
- A glass of squash
- A cup of tea
- A pint of lager
- A slice of orange

In this example, three of the alternatives provide a less expensive solution. Some of the alternatives provide thirst quenching and some other benefits that go beyond what the person is asking. By asking the questions, you may design a better, cheaper or less time-consuming offer.

Planned or unplanned?

"Organisations that are completely reactive about their analysis will do nothing until something goes wrong or stops being effective, at which point, of course, it may be too late. They will always be following the pack when it comes to learning and development."[18]

The question then is whether you, in your L&D department, want to be behind the pack, whether you want to take a reactive or proactive approach, and who will make that decision. There are some occasions when a needs analysis cannot be planned and so it is important that we consider the difference between these two approaches, because it may influence how we respond to any suggestion of a learning need.

For example, if we take the example of the loss of a major customer, which I cannot imagine anyone ever plans, the shock of the loss could cause panic in the organisation. That panic may lead to rash decisions, laying of blame and desperate attempts to regain market share in other ways. A reactive, knee-jerk response then leads to mass training interventions to address the problem that caused the loss.

"At one end of the spectrum is the proactive, planned pressure of business or corporate strategy... At the other end is the knee-jerk reaction to unforeseen and unexpected pressures."[5]

What may be useful to consider, as part of your L&D strategy, is having a plan for how L&D responds to such unplanned events. Having a plan of reflection and analysis before action may prevent wasting even more money on training or learning interventions that – at best – solve a problem that has caused the loss of one major customer, but at worse could distract your organisation from concentrating on its primary focus.

Considering how to approach planned needs analysis as part of your strategy can also give insight on the budget and resources you will need. This considered approach elicits greater appreciation by the organisation that L&D is a credible business partner, not just a learning purveyor.

Frances and Roland Bee, authors of *Learning Needs Analysis and Evaluation* have been working as consultants in L&D for many years in their own consultancy, and in Frances' case, for the CIPD. Bee and Bee mention that "...we see the business needs of organisations as not just the starting point for any Learning Needs Analysis but the force that should be driving and learning interventions." If we take this as being true, then needs analysis should be a major part of any L&D strategy.

Once you have completed this chapter, you may find it easier to add a way to handle needs analysis, planned or unplanned, to your learning strategy. The table below shows examples of when needs analysis can be planned and when it cannot.

Planned	**Unplanned**
Entry into new markets	Loss of major customer
Annual collation of appraisal information	Sudden departure of a key employee
New product launch	Sudden rise in complaints
New manager being promoted	Sudden rise in accidents
New customer service standard launch	Sudden drop in productivity
Introduction of a new process or online system	Grievance procedure instigated on a manager

Levels of needs analysis

When planning a needs analysis and the resources required to undertake it, you need to determine the level at which you should conduct that analysis. If the analysis is just for one person, planning will be a simple effort: maybe using some standard departmental tools. If the analysis is for a group with influence and impact in the organisation (say, the senior team), more planning and discussions about different perspectives will be required. The higher the associated impact of the people who need performance issues addressing, the more thought needs to go into how to drill down into those needs. To identify with clarity, the perceived needs of a group, you need to take several perspectives as in the *triangulation approach*[13] so that any skewed perceptions, may be identified by cross-checking with others. We will discuss triangulation later in this chapter.

Occupational

This is a generic needs analysis relating to job roles. It may be performed as part of advance-planning the specific job roles required, so that you can have a blend of learning solutions available, maybe on your learning management system or using subject matter experts within the organisation.

"Occupational assessment examines the skills, knowledge and abilities required for affected occupational groups. Occupational assessment identifies how and which occupational discrepancies or gaps exist, potentially introduced by the new direction of an agency. It also examines new ways to do work that can eliminate the discrepancies or gaps."[5]

This type of analysis is more likely to happen in larger organisations where there are well-defined roles and teams. It may also happen in matrix structures, where roles are flexible and it is unlikely that any new person hired will have the exact experience or knowledge required. That flexible approach means that people may have to learn on the job in a just-in-time fashion. Knowing how learning might be achieved will help in curating resources.

In a matrix structure, the job role analysis is likely to evolve with time and should be reaffirmed periodically.

Individual

Although this may seem obvious, an individual needs analysis will be performed for a specific person within the organisation. If you are struggling to differentiate between this and the job role one, the individual one will have a person's name on it and not just a job title.

"Individual assessment analyses how well an individual employee is doing a job and determines the individual's capacity to do new or different work. Individual assessment provides information on which employees need training and what kind."[5]

If you have already done needs analysis for a job role then it may be quite simple to tweak this for an individual. For example, you may have a needs analysis for a customer representative in a call centre in an organisation that has many call centres, each dealing with different services and products. For the individual starting in the call centre specifically dealing with complaints, however, there will be a different emphasis on some aspects of the role. For example:

- Listening and communication skills at an advanced level to deal with people who are in an agitated state

- A self-reliant attitude and an ability to bounce back
- A calm nature with the ability to focus in on the nub of the problem.

In summary, an individual needs analysis will be much more specific than the generic job role one.

Departmental or Team

On occasions, all the members of a team will have the same roles as each other and so the type of needs analysis will be the same as the job role one. However, if we consider a finance department as a whole, the skills and knowledge required may be various:

- Accounting methods
- Finance regulations (own country and abroad)
- Commercial awareness
- Audit project management
- Tax and National Insurance
- Accounting software
- Attention to detail
- Analytical skills

In a large organisation, there may be 30 people or more required to have these skills, but with a narrow remit for each team member. Therefore, for a finance team, the needs analysis may yield the same results as for a smaller team, but the individual knowledge and skills requirements would be broader in the smaller team.

Organisational

The reasons why you may have to do an organisation-wide needs analysis may vary:

- Change of direction in terms of products and services
- A buyout from another company
- A new company facing rapid growth
- Radical changes in legislation

For the last one, an example might be the latest (2018) GDPR (General Data Protection Regulations) legislation. The legislation has far-reaching impacts on all businesses, but not everyone in an organisation may need to understand it and implement it to the same level. Consider the level of understanding and application of the GDPR for these roles:

- Chief Financial Officer
- Head of Sales and Marketing
- Administrators that look after and clean client records
- Client-facing servers in the call centre

Suffice to say that each one will need a slightly different level of knowledge and application to the other.

"Organizational assessment evaluates the level of organizational performance. An assessment of this type will determine what skills knowledge and abilities an agency needs. It determines what is required to alleviate the problems and weaknesses of the agency as well as to enhance strengths and competencies, especially for Mission Critical Occupations (MCO). Organizational assessment takes into consideration various additional factors, including changing demographics, political trends, technology and the economy."[5]

Objectives 2.2 and 2.3

This activity will help you decide at what level an analysis should be conducted as well as determining if it can be planned

LNA Methods

(See Appendix A for more details on these learning needs analysis methods.)

Organisational	Departmental/Team	Individual	Job Role
Records checking – complaints, MI, waste	Quality checks	Assessment centre	Job analysis
Implementation of projects	Focus groups	Questionnaires	Hierarchical task analysis
Analysis of corporate mission and strategic plans	Critical Incident technique	Interview	Succession planning
Critical Incident technique*	Competency framework	Identification of own needs	Manpower planning
SWOT	Analysis of departmental plans	Observation	SWOT
	Analysis of appraisals	Work sampling	Focus group
Focus groups	Implementation of projects	Testing	
Analysis of appraisals	SWOT	Hierarchical task* analysis	
	Interview team	Quality checks	
	360 feedback	Job analysis*	
		Scoring grid	
	Psychometric tests	SWOT	
	Workshop	Analysis of appraisals	
		360 feedback	
		Psychometric tests	
		Simulations	
		Reflective exercise	

Above is a table of different LNA methods categorised into Organisational, Departmental, Individual and Job Role so that you are able to choose according to the levels of analysis we've just seen. This is by no means an exhaustive list. Each of these methods should be considered in terms of:

- The specific project you are working on and what impact it will have on the organisation (the more impactful it is, the more careful your consideration of how you will analyse the needs)
- Your budget
- Your resources
- The time you have

ACTIVITY

Objective 2.4

Now that you have a better idea of the methods available to you to conduct a needs analysis and some indicators as to when these might be suitable, it seems a good place to see if you can apply this. This activity will help you see how to make the right selection for your situation.

Before we do this, let me continue the story I began in Chapter 1.

Case Study Part 2

I had submitted a proposal to the client to conduct a detailed needs analysis on a group of team leaders. In the proposal, I needed to outline how long the analysis would take and also which methods I would be using. Let me explain my thinking behind why I chose the methods I did.

During the conversation with the MD, he mentioned on many occasions what the senior team thought of their team leaders. There were not many complimentary things said, apart from when they spoke about the two newest team leaders, that they had recruited recently. This was a departure for them, as most of the team leaders had been promoted into their roles.

One of the team leaders in particular was a 'problem'. His behaviour was unprofessional at times and he did not get on with a lot of the other team leaders. All the little anecdotes fed into my thinking, *What else do I need to know?* Asking myself this helped me decide how I could further inform some of the questions bubbling in my mind.

The original 'shopping list' of training that I was called in to quote for was as follows:

- Managing conflict with others
- Time management for leaders
- Presentation skills
- Meeting skills
- Delegation skills
- Problem solving

For me, some of the questions that needed answering were:

- How much conflict was going on?
- What was it about?
- What did they do when conflict arose?
- What did they not do?
- What made the MD and the senior team think they could not manage their time, problem-solve or delegate?
- What sort of problems were they asked to solve?

I knew that I needed to get together with the senior team to find out more about their perception of this group of team leaders. I also needed to know what their expectations were, in the context of what the organisation wanted to achieve.

I wanted to know more about the organisation, its aspirations and goals. I desperately wanted to hear what the team leaders had to say. So, I chose three methods as part of this needs analysis:

- Desk research on the company, reading:
  - The induction pack for new starters (containing vision, mission, corporate goals)
  - Brochures and any literature describing the organisation to their customers
  - Team leader job specification – used to create a set of competencies for team leaders which the SMT could rank in order of importance
- A face-to-face workshop with the senior team to elicit:
  - What their ideal team leader would be like
  - Where the current team leaders were at present
  - Anything else they felt important to the development of the company as a whole
- A survey to the team leaders (15 in total) to compare what their senior managers were saying about them and what they thought about themselves. A comparison of the two perspectives might reveal more than I anticipated! The survey would be completed and delivered after the meeting with the senior managers.

My justification for meeting with the senior team was that there were only 6 of them and so capturing their opinions would be fairly straightforward. As there were 15 of the team leaders, a survey, carefully worded, would be the easiest way to compare their opinions against the senior managers'.

Selecting appropriate needs analysis methods

Reading this part of the case study should give you some insights into how to decide which methods are appropriate. In general, they have to be:

- Answering the questions still in your head
- Not taking up too much time or resource
- Giving you a best estimate of the whole picture

Bear in mind you will never know *all* that is going on or not happening. Choosing three different perspectives will give you a fuller picture but not a perfect one. This is called a *triangulation approach* and is best described as "a vehicle for cross-validation when two or more distinct methods are found to be congruent and yield comparable data"[13]. Or in other words, the ability to check data you have collected is true by using other data to verify or validate it.

 ACTIVITY

Objective 2.5

In this activity, you will look at three different scenarios and choose three different methods to approach the LNA.

When selecting a range of methods for any analysis, bear in mind the questions that you need to answer. Once you have these in your head, write them down and place them in the order you need to answer them. Selecting the first method may lead you to consider what you might do with the information you gain from that first stage to feed it into the second stage and so on. If you have previously thought that any needs analysis had to be planned to the letter before beginning, consider that the data may inform the next stage of the analysis as you go and therefore require some tweaking.

Case Study Part 3

Looking at the organisational plans and induction packs helped me to understand more about the aspirations of the organisation and prepared me for the workshop with the senior team. It informed the questions I asked and also allowed me to challenge certain assumptions they made during that workshop. Their answers then informed me in designing the survey I sent out to the team leaders, including a question on how much time the team leaders spent with their senior managers – enough, too much or not enough? You may have a plan for the analysis, but with each new input of information, you should be prepared to adjust how exactly you execute it in the end.

Planning a needs analysis

You may or may not have done many needs analyses and I hope you're at the point where you see a strong case for doing them. There is a strong case for ensuring that they become part of your routine work in L&D. Here's why. If an analysis is not conducted beforehand, Raymond Noe[4] speaks about how:

- "Training may be incorrectly used as a solution to a performance problem (when the solution should deal with employee motivation, job design, or a better communication of performance expectations).
- Training programs may have the wrong content, objectives, or methods.
- Trainees may be sent to training programs for which they do not have the basic skills, prerequisite skills, or confidence needed to learn.
- Training will not deliver the expected learning, behaviour change, or financial results that the company expects.
- Money will be spent on training programs that are unnecessary because they are unrelated to the company's business strategy." [4]

In Noe's research, he shows "three critical areas that bridge the gap between learning events and on-the-job performance. These are: improving needs analysis, building learner motivation and enabling manager support."[4]

Even when something unexpected happens and you have to do a needs analysis, you do not have to be caught unaware. You can have a contingency plan for what to do in case of something happening that is critical to the business. The questions you will ask yourself for a planned or unplanned needs analysis are:

- How much time do we have for the analysis?
- Which stakeholders are supporting the analysis? Who will be involved?
- How much budget is there?
- What resources or methods do we have at our disposal? (This list should be assembled in any case so that you are not always going to the same methods.)
- Which three perspectives do we need to look at?
- In what order will we look into the information?
- Who will be helping with the data-gathering and analysis?

ACTIVITY

Objective 2.6

Create your own plan for a project you are embarking on or a plan for something unexpected happening where you would want to have time to reflect before action.

Use the worksheet to gather information about who would sponsor and support the needs analysis and look at the spreadsheet to see what a simple timeline might look like for a project such as this.

In this chapter, you have had a chance to consider if a deeper analysis is warranted for a project you are undertaking as well as looking at some of the methods that you might choose for a needs analysis. Go through the activities to meet the objectives below and get closer to understanding how you not only get closer to the business but provide value in what you do.

Just a quick recap of what you have covered in this chapter and what you should be able to do:

Objectives:

2.1 Describe situations where an in-depth analysis is or is not required.
Completed (date and sign)..

2.2 Differentiate between a planned and unplanned needs analysis.
Completed (date and sign)..

2.3 Categorise correctly the level of needs analysis to be undertaken.
Completed (date and sign)..

2.4 List some appropriate methods for analysing needs for groups and individuals.
Completed (date and sign)..

2.5 With the use of notes, choose a triangulation approach to needs analysis by selecting three methods for some given case studies.
Completed (date and sign)..

2.6 Put together a plan for conducting an analysis, including time and resources required.
Completed (date and sign)..

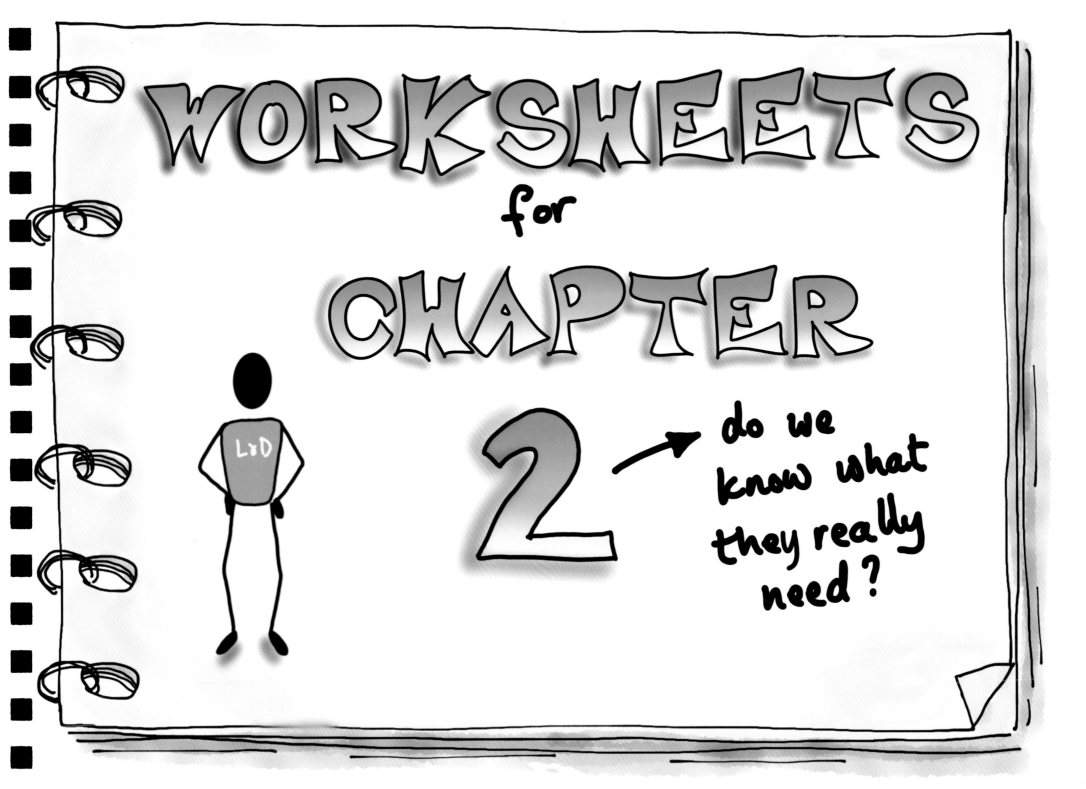

2.1 Checklist
Is a deeper analysis needed?

Before you embark on a design or delivery check to make sure you have the following:

1	Clear organisational requirement	
2	Clear team/individual requirement in line with what the organisational goals are	
3	Clear measures of success	
4	Stakeholder(s) owns the measures of success and is willing to measure	
5	Stakeholder(s) willing to imbed learning and do follow up activities	
6	Clear knowledge type learning outcomes and level (according to Blooms taxonomy)	
7	Clear skills type learning outcomes and level (according to Blooms taxonomy)	
8	Clear attitudinal learning outcomes and level (according to Blooms taxonomy)	
9	Clarity on the gaps in knowledge, skills or behaviours	
10	Assurance that this is a learning need and not any other underlying issue	

2.2 2.3 Needs Analysis Case Studies

Consider these case studies and determine:

- The level of the needs analysis (organisational, departmental/team, individual or job role)
- Whether this could be planned or whether it would be unplanned

1. Introduction of a new absence management system

Level

Planned or unplanned?

2. An individual instigates a grievance against their line manager for bullying

Level

Planned or unplanned?

3. The appointment of a new manager into a new post in the organisation

Level

Planned or unplanned?

4. Introduction of a new payroll system

Level

Planned or unplanned?

Needs Analysis Case Studies – answers

1. Introduction of a new absence management system
   Level – Organisational. Managers will need different training to staff. Staff will need to be aware of system and how to book in sick, but managers will need to know how to administer.
   Foreseen or Fire fighting – Foreseen, planned carefully with an end date in mind for implementation

2. An individual instigates a grievance against their line manager for bullying
   Level – Individual. The manager may have had appropriate training, but is it their attitude that is lacking?
   Foreseen or fire fighting? – Cannot be planned for, especially if equal opportunities training is already given to all managers on a regular basis.

3. The appointment of a new manager into a new post in the organisation
   Level – job role. The job specification will determine which learning needs the new individual will need
   Foreseen or fire fighting? – Foreseen. The post should be planned and should be part of a larger strategy

4. Introduction of a new payroll system
   Level – departmental. Will only affect the payroll dept
   Foreseen or fire fighting? – Foreseen, planned roll out of new system

2.4 LNA Methods

This activity will help you think about which methods may be suitable in different circumstances and according to your budget. You will be organising the given methods into categories: High/Low cost and whether they are suitable for a group or an individual.

1. Take a piece of flipchart paper and divide it in 4 sections as in the diagram below

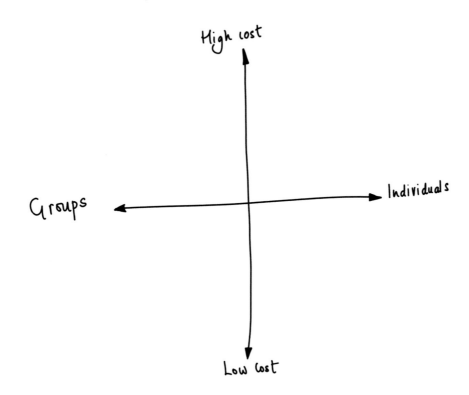

2. Looking at each of the methods in the table, decide where on the grid it should be placed. It may sit in more than one quadrant

Needs Analysis Methods	
360 feedback	Observation
Analyse corporate mission and strategic plans	Psychometric tests
Analyse departmental plans	Quality checks
Analysis of appraisals (performance reviews)	Questionnaires
Assessment centre	Records checking – complaints, MI, waste
Critical Incident technique	Reflective exercise
Competency framework	Scoring Grid
Focus groups	Simulations
Hierarchical task analysis	Stakeholder conversation
Identification of own needs	Succession planning
Implementation of projects	SWOT
Interview	Testing
Job analysis	Workshop
Manpower planning	Work sampling

2.4 LNA Methods Answers

Group (High cost)	Individual (High cost)
360 feedback Assessment centre Analysis of appraisals Critical Incident technique Competency framework Focus group Interviews Implementation of projects Manpower planning Succession planning	360 feedback Assessment centre Hierarchical task analysis Interviews Job analysis Testing Succession planning Work sampling
Group (Low cost)	**Individual (Low cost)**
Analyse corporate mission and strategic plans Analyse departmental plans Identification of own needs Critical Incident technique SWOT Analyse departmental plans Quality checks	Quality checks Analysis of appraisals Identification of own needs Implementation of projects Observation Questionnaires SWOT Scoring Grid

2.5 LNA Case Studies

For each of these scenarios, consider, how you might dig deeper to do a more thorough analysis. Choose three methods that may help answer the questions that are bubbling in your head, because the brief is so brief. Consider not only the people involved, but those affected by the things that are going on when choosing your methods.

1. Customer complaints begin to rise in the customer service team as a whole and no one seems to know the real cause. Some people, though not all, have been struggling with some of the online tools. How would you begin an analysis to uncover what is going on behind the scenes? Which methods would you choose?

What are the questions bubbling in your head?	
LNA Method 1	
LNA Method 2	
LNA Method 3	

2. A new team member arrives, who you know has not got all the relevant experience required but has a great "can-do" attitude and a real willingness to learn. How could you get an accurate picture of what they need to learn to get to speed quickly?

What are the questions bubbling in your head?	
LNA Method 1	
LNA Method 2	
LNA Method 3	

3. Your organisation is about to move into new markets by buying out an existing company. Most of the staff will be kept on and you have plans to expand the market share, so will need some of your staff to gain new skills in this area. You will probably need to recruit more staff too in order to serve the geographical areas you wish to cover.

What are the questions bubbling in your head?	
LNA Method 1	
LNA Method 2	
LNA Method 3	

1.5 LNA Case Studies Answers

For each of these scenarios, consider, how you might dig deeper to do a more thorough analysis. Choose three methods that may help answer the questions that are bubbling in your head, because the brief is so brief. Consider not only the people involved, but those affected by the things that are going on when choosing your methods.

1. Customer complaints begin to rise in the customer service team (45 people) as a whole and no one seems to know the real cause. Some people, though not all, have been struggling with some of the online tools. How would you begin an analysis to uncover what is going on behind the scenes? Which methods would you choose?

Questions:

- *What are the most common types of complaints?*
- *Are they the same as previously or are they a new type of complaint?*
- *Are the complaints for everyone or just specific people?*
- *What do the new tools do?*

What might begin to uncover the answers is looking more closely at:

I. *Existing complaints data – how many over time, nature of the complaint, who the complaint was about, data spanning a time before the complaints went up*

II. *Select some of the customers highlighted in the data above and speak with them on the phone to get more information about what went wrong*

III. *As the team is quite large, a survey might be a good way to get their opinions on some of the tools they are using. Need to find out whether the tools are at fault or if it is a lack of experience in using them.*

2. A new team member arrives into the finance team, who you know has not got all the relevant experience required but has a great "can-do" attitude and a real willingness to learn. How could you get an accurate picture of what they need to learn to get up to speed quickly?

Questions:
- *Who recruited them and why?*
- *Is the role an existing or new one?*
- *What are their strengths and weaknesses?*
- *Have they had any feedback so far?*
- *What do they want to achieve and what would stop them?*

Some possible methods of needs analysis might be:
    I.   *Do a job analysis using the job specification used to recruit them with their recruiter to get an accurate picture of what is required*
    II.   *Complete a scoring grid, to show how important each part of the role is, using the results from above*
    III.   *Get the person to do a SWOT analysis on themselves using a combination of the job analysis and the scoring grid**
       *Quite often when you embark on a needs analysis, the first stage will feed into the next and so on.

3. Your organisation is about to move into new markets by buying out an existing company. Most of the staff will be kept on and you have plans to expand the market share, so will need some of your staff to gain new skills in this area. You will probably need to recruit more staff too in order to serve the geographical areas you wish to cover.

Questions:
- *How many staff old and new with the skills required?*
- *To what level do these skills need to be?*
- *Are there any experts in the whole pool of staff?*
- *In which geographic areas are the staff at the moment and how many will need to be recruited and where?*

Methods of needs analysis:
I. *Look at HR records to find out about where the staff are located*
II. *Make contact with L&D in the other company to find out if they have a skills or competency matrix to check which skills are needed*
III. *Use the records above to survey the new and existing staff about their perceived level of expertise I the new markets.*

2.6 Needs Analysis Preparation

Title	
Date	
Analysis lead	
Team members involved	
Main sponsor	
Other stakeholders	

Start date		End date
Budget		

Resources or methods to be considered	*Online surveys, assessment centre etc*	Approved?
Perspectives to be considered	*Customers, Head of Sales, etc*	Rating 1=not important 6= very important

Needs analysis methods chosen		Notes
Method 1		
Method 2		
Method 3		

84

2.6 Needs Project Plan

Project name	21/03/2019	28/03/2019	04/04/2019	11/04/2019	18/04/2019	25/04/2019	02/05/2019	09/05/2019	16/05/2019	23/05/2019
Initial scoping of project	X									
Kick off meeting		X								
Prep work sent for managers 4/4/19		X	X							
Meet senior managers 13/4/19				X						
Desk research		X	X	X						
Create survey outline for team leaders				X	X					
Send out survey 25/4/19						X				
Deadline for survey 6/5/19							X			
Analyse data								X	X	
Complete report and present								X	X	X

Collecting and interpreting the information

Objectives:

By the end of the chapter, you will be able to:

3.1 Differentiate between the 'gut feelings' you have experienced in past decisions you have made and the more analytical approach.

3.2 Describe why it is important to collect data.

3.3 Relate what you do to what the organisational goals are.

3.4 Define some key measures for your role in line with organisational requirements.

3.5 Differentiate between data and information.

3.6 Differentiate between qualitative and quantitative data.

3.7 Choose for three case studies, the format the data will take.

3.8 Describe what you need to do before you start collecting your data.

In this chapter, we will be getting to the analytics part.

"Learning analytics is the science and art of gathering, processing, interpreting and reporting data related to the efficiency, effectiveness and business impact of development programmes designed to improve individual and organizational performance and inform stakeholders."[5]

In my opinion, this could be before any learning takes place to inform any decisions about the actions that are required to plug a performance gap. Equally, it could be after learning has taken place to measure the impact.

The part your instincts play

When collecting data and performing any sort of analysis, there are a few factors to consider:

- Organisations are complex systems with many influences and variables.
- Changing one area of the system can affect many other areas or none at all.
- Where a simple relationship exists in one organisation between one statistic and another, the same cannot be said for every organisation.

The reason for sharing these insights is to assure you that *data* cannot be the whole answer to the questions you are asking. At some point, you will turn the data into *information* and use it – to the best of your ability – to inform your decisions.

Our ability to make good decisions comes from what we might call 'intuition' and some information to back up that choice. Intuition itself has been researched (CIPD 2014) and those found to have great insights and make good decisions quickly are practiced in doing so[14].They have gone through the process of questioning, data-gathering, sense-making, interpreting that information and applying it to their situation many times. They have honed these skills so much that, on occasions, they can skip the data-gathering and get a 'gut feel' as to the solution to a problem.

Anyone who has worked in an industry long enough will begin to develop a 'gut feeling' for what is (or is not) going on. Their ability to sense what is happening will improve with time. Some people develop this skill faster than others and some need to go through that process of data-gathering, sense-making, checking and validating to gain enough confidence to listen to their instincts.

That said, should we only go by what our instincts are telling us? If I had a simple answer to that then this book would sell out in no time. What I might suggest is:

- If you lack confidence and experience, use information to inform your decision-making, while trying to sense what might be happening. Reflect on what you thought were the underlying problems and compare to what you found them to be through analysis.
- If you have experience and confidence in your gut instinct, periodically check in to that instinct by using solid information to back it up.
- When your gut instinct is saying 'no', but the information says 'go', do not ignore your gut. Double check the data sources you used. If you have used three, for example, try a fourth to get confirmation.
- When the information says 'no', but your gut says 'go', ask yourself what may be behind your gut feeling. Could it be some bias or desire driving that feeling? Could it be a time pressure from elsewhere driving you to make a hasty decision?

As I mentioned in Chapter 1, my background in engineering has shaped my approach to learning and development. Skills I learned as a young engineer have stood me in good stead as a professional in a field that does not always rely on a scientific approach in decision-making.

Let me share a few short anecdotes that may surprise you about your fundamental beliefs surrounding engineering. You may think that every decision an engineer makes must be backed by maths, physics or some scientific formula. Yet I have seen the importance of instinct on many occasions in my engineering career.

As a fuel technologist, I was often asked if a specific coal would be suitable for converting a particular oil-fired boiler to coal-firing. I would look at the technical drawings of the boiler, determine if there were any tight bends that the combustion gases had to navigate and if the ash content of the coal proposed would cause slag to form on those bends. Slag build-up could have catastrophic consequences on the running of a boiler; hence needing a sense of whether the combination of that coal with that boiler would work. If the answer was yes, then I could go on to run short trials to confirm my suspicions. If the answer was no (based on past experience), I could propose a different coal, just to be on the safe side.

As a meteorologist, working in a company that manufactured wind turbines, my role was twofold:

- To collect and analyse data from prospective and existing sites
- To find the best place on a site to position the wind turbines.

Data collected on prospective sites could be extrapolated to determine if it was windy enough to justify the expense of a turbine. The hourly variation of the wind speed and the topography (from a map and site visit) would allow me to judge if the prevailing wind was too inconsistent or likely to cause unbearable stresses on the turbine blades.

Data collected from existing sites and the subsequent power output from the wind turbines would confirm initial estimates. The more often I went through this process of data collection, siting and then further data collection, the better I became at judging the suitability of a site. After a while, just looking at a map or visiting a site, my gut feeling would be enough to make the determination about where to situate a wind turbine. Though I can't say I was ever confident (or foolish!) enough to do so.

If you're reading this book, thinking you have to abandon any sense of intuition in favour of collecting data, I hope you have been reassured. And if you firmly believe that all decisions should be driven through analysis, I hope there is a little room for you to explore the development of your own intuition.

ACTIVITY

Objective 3.1

Reflect on a past project that went really well or really badly. Use the reflection sheet to test your instinct and how it was at work in that situation. Reflect on how you might have done things differently and also where you measure up on the scale from instinctive to data-driven.

Why collect data anyway?

Before we move onto what form data may take, let's pause to consider why we are collecting it in the first place. "Business leaders are calling upon HR to move from reporting analytics; from using data to provide talent reports to using analytics to improve business decisions."[5]

This also applies to L&D as "64% of CEOs cite building a skilled workforce as a top priority and 77% of heads of L&D report an increase in demands from the business to demonstrate business impact."[5]

"Only 12% of CFOs are confident or highly confident that HR and L&D are spending the right amounts in the right places. Only 23% of line leaders agree or strongly agree that they are satisfied with the overall effectiveness of the L&D function."[5]

"According to the ROI Institute, the information that business leaders want focuses on the following three areas:

- Application: how can we increase application of new skills on the job?
- Results: to what degree will a learning programme improve a specific business outcome?
- Value: what will be the return on the learning investment?"[5]

All of the above are pretty compelling reasons why not only should L&D collect data, but also that it must focus on measuring the impact on performance rather than any metric which may not indicate any improvements in the way the organisation runs, however small.

When I joined IBM as an instructor in the late 80s, my role was to train people in the VM systems user interface. The goal was to improve the skills of the participants on the system, with the ultimate aim of boosting their performance at work.

Definition: *education* (noun)

1. *The process of receiving or giving systematic instruction, especially at a school or university.*
2. *An enlightening experience.*

Prior to that, my experiences in learning were from an academic perspective: I was educated at school and that education prepared me for the world in so many different ways. There was not always a specific purpose to the learning, but overall it served to shape and form me into the person I have become. To me, that is education. And it has a broader and more long-term perspective.

In my opinion, learning, in the context of an organisation that requires people to perform in some way and strive for improvements in their performance, differs slightly to education. So, keep an open mind as I elaborate on this one. Some may disagree with me but hear me out...

Having identified areas where there are gaps in performance, the purpose of learning would be to trigger the *improvements required*, quite simply. That said, if you introduce certain things in the 'learning' as part of their wider 'education', you may indeed inspire people to want to learn and improve more.

This can be the dilemma in learning: time to devote to learning for your role is precious and there are an ever-increasing number of priorities. We devise more and more ways to deliver the learning in an increasingly efficient way: e-learning, micro-learning, mobile learning etc. Have we forgotten how to inspire people to want to learn more about the subject and become obsessed with the medium in which we deliver it? Could we argue that sometimes taking a little more time on learning will save time in the long run, because people will be more motivated to learn? Or do we just need to make learning specific to a role and delivered in the most timely and efficient way to ensure great performance on the job? We could probably spend a whole week debating this one!

Assume for now that the purpose of learning is solely to improve performance to help the organisation survive and thrive. That being the case, collecting data will help us determine whether people are surviving or thriving, which aspects of performance need to improve and what can be done about them. Ultimately, the purpose of L&D is to align more closely to the organisation.

"In its simplest form, alignment involves measuring a business unit's strengths and performance gaps at an individual level by gathering and analysing data and then filling those gaps with highly targeted learning solutions."[5]

"In an article published in 2014 in *T+D Magazine*, Diane Valenti recommends four questions to align development programmes with strategic objectives. Those questions are:

- What is the organization's goal for the coming fiscal year?
- What tactics do you plan to employ to achieve this goal?
- Who will be implementing these tactics?
- What new knowledge and/or skills do you anticipate they will need to implement these tactics?"[5]

There are three critical areas that bridge the gap between learning events and on-the-job performance. These are: improving needs analysis, building learner motivation and enabling manager support. Improving learning needs analysis leads to a 29% improvement in learner performance in relation to critical business objectives.[5]

In a small organisation, roles may be more fluid than in a larger one. There may be more crossover between what individuals are required to do to allow for absence or a lack of people to fill every role. When you were interviewed for your current role, it may have been perfectly clear from the job description what you would be required to do. With time, that can change in any role and there seems to be an inevitable drift away from what your original purpose was when first hired to where you are now.

ACTIVITY

Objective 3.2

Reflect on why it is important for you to collect data from different perspectives:
- Yours
- Your team and manager
- The organisation

This activity will show you the link your role has to what the organisation is trying to achieve, as well as identifying key measures (or someone else's). Look at your job description (if still relevant) and consider these questions:

- What are the three key things that you are required to *do* in your role?
- How do you know if you are doing those things well? Be specific in how you would measure this.
- How does what you do relate to what the organisation is trying to achieve?
- What could you do better to improve what the organisation does?

ACTIVITY

Objective 3.3 and 3.4

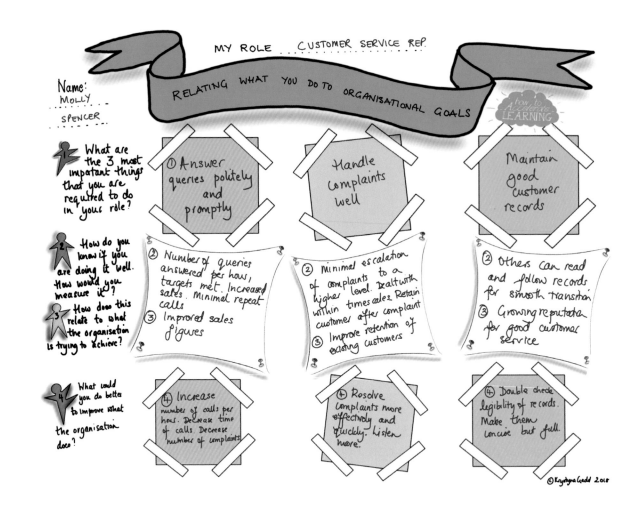

Looking at the figure below, you could collect data to inform your decision-making and improve performance for the customer service representative:

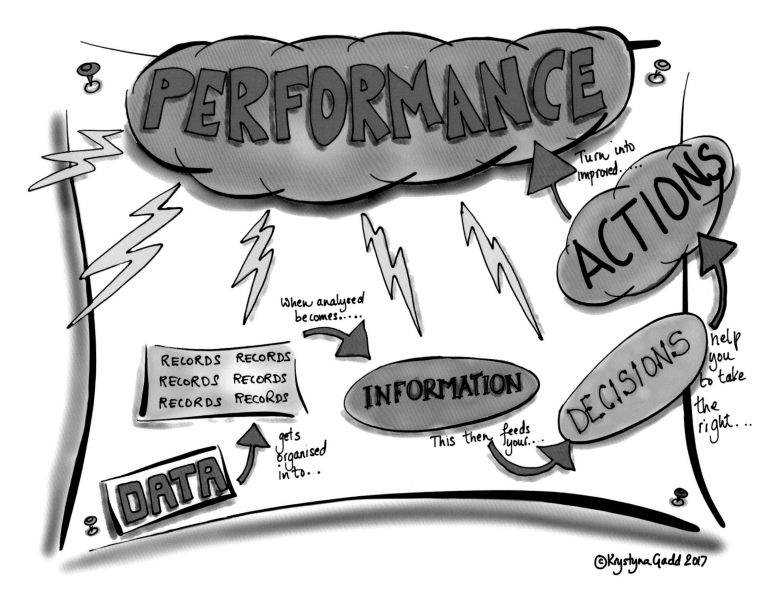

Specifically, how this relates to the customer service representative can be seen in the next diagram:

95

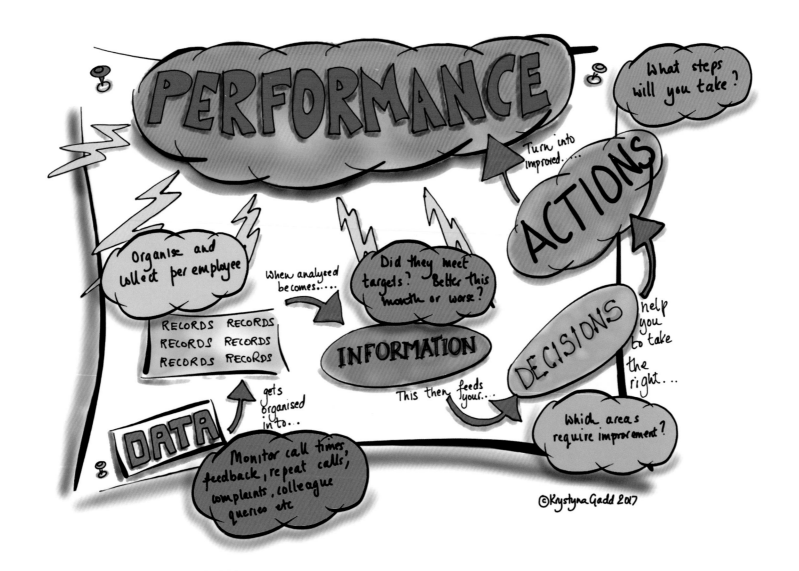

ACTIVITY

Objective 3.5

Looking at the worksheet, match the examples with the terms.

Making life easier when collecting data

Before deciding which needs analysis methods you are going to use, it may be prudent to consider the format of the data you will get back, as this may determine the methods you use. Remember, the more paper you have to sort and transfer to a spreadsheet, the more work for you and your team. Some tips on data formats:

- If it's electronic, find out if there is a reporting facility, or the data can be transferred easily to a spreadsheet.
- If data is collected on paper, do not assume that this will always be difficult. Prepare parts that are scales and ratings, so you have numbers to play with in a spreadsheet, with some free-form comments.
- Free-form comments are good, but not always easy to compare one against the other. (It's not impossible, but consider a mixture.)
- Recognise the difference between quantitative and qualitative data formats.

Qualitative

"Qualitative information is less absolute and more about qualities."[18] Data that approximates or characterises but does not measure the attributes, characteristics, properties, and so on of a thing or phenomenon. Qualitative data describes whereas quantitative data defines.

97

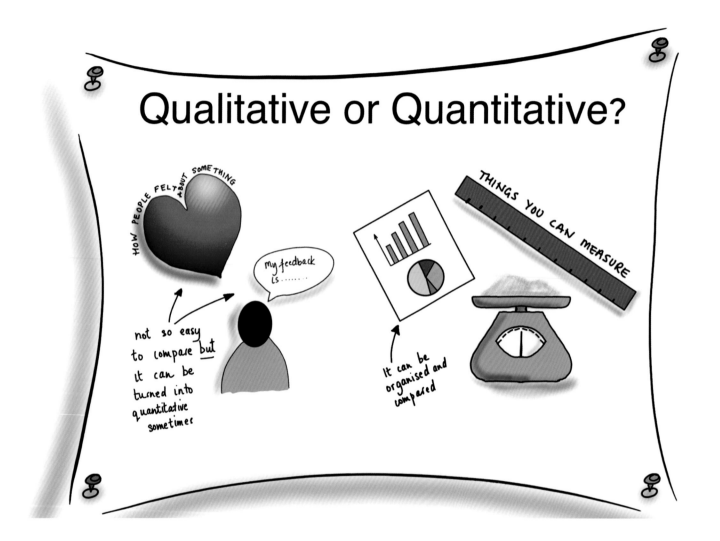

Quantitative

"Quantitative data is about facts, things that can be measured."[18] Data that can be quantified and verified and is amenable to statistical manipulation. Quantitative data defines whereas qualitative data describes.

Objective 3.6

Looking at the worksheet, sort out the data into qualitative (more to do with feelings (F)) or quantitative (to do with numbers (N)).

These seem to be pretty clear-cut definitions and yet there are ways to collect qualitative data, in which people express their opinions, that you can analyse to make it more quantitative. Let me give you an example from the evaluation form I use:

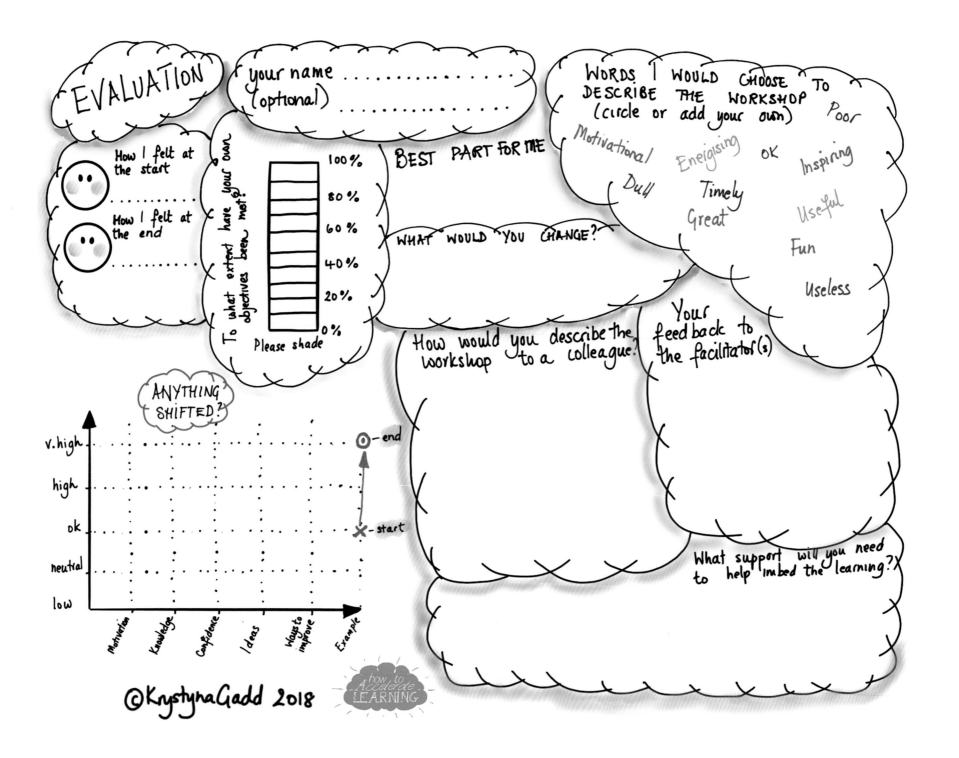

Although most of this evaluation sheet is collecting qualitative and subjective data, let us see how this can be made more quantitative:

- 'Anything shifted'
    - When analysed, 100% of participants stated something had shifted as a result of the learning.
    - The largest shifts were in an increase in motivation and ideas.
- 'Words to describe'
    - 100% of the words used to describe the event were positive.
    - The most frequently used word was 'inspiring'.
- 'Best part for me'
    - 40% quoted that the best part was the last activity and 30% quoted it was the activity on objective-setting.
- 'Support needed'
    - 80% suggested the support needed was going to be from their line manager.

The last point, 'support needed', emphasises that it takes effort to embed learning and improve performance.

"One study investigated a variety of roles that managers play in the learning and performance process. Five were measured linked to performance:

- evaluating learner readiness before attending trainings
- setting expectations for learning before training begins
- getting involved with application of training after the learner attends
- following up on expectations that were set before training
- providing necessary resources to support performance."[5]

Appendix A of this book lists LNA Methods according to their suitability to level and also whether they provide qualitative or quantitative data. Quantitative data is easier to analyse and manipulate into tables and graphs. If you need to analyse the needs of large groups, you'll require a mixture of both. Quantitative data, though easy to analyse and spot patterns, similarities and differences, may open up many questions as to what might be happening. Qualitative data, which will be more free-form, may provide answers to those questions or clues as to what might be behind any anomalies.

Objective 3.7

For the case studies in the activity for Objective 2.5, describe what format the data you collect will take. Will it be qualitative or quantitative?

Case Study Part 4

Going back to our case study, here's how data formats can apply to a real-life situation.

After meeting with the senior team and reflecting on the information gathered, further questions arose in my mind. I circulated some of these to the senior managers and collated their responses, then summarised them to describe the themes emerging:

- Did they really need time management training or did they just not have time because they were not delegating?
- Does the company need managers or leaders?

Some of the data collected from the team leaders in respect of how they ranked themselves against the team leader competencies conflicted with how the senior leaders saw them. The free-form comments from the team leaders therefore helped to provide further clues as to what the disconnect may be.

What you need to do before collecting data

Let's rewind and remember an important point: the whole reason we are collecting and analysing data is to help people perform better. In learning and development, we may be mistaken that our role is to help people to learn better. We might not at times make the connection as to why they may *need* to learn better – and that is to perform better!

"According to the ROI Institute, the information that business leaders want focuses on the following three areas:

- Application: how can we increase application of new skills on the job?
- Results: to what degree will a learning programme improve a specific business outcome?
- Value: what will be the return on the learning investment?"[5]

The role of the modern learning leader has been evolving and I have been inspired by the work being undertaken by Towards Maturity in *Driving the New Learning Organisation* (see diagram below). At the centre is Clarity of Purpose, a real sense of knowing where the organisation is heading and how it will know that it is getting there.

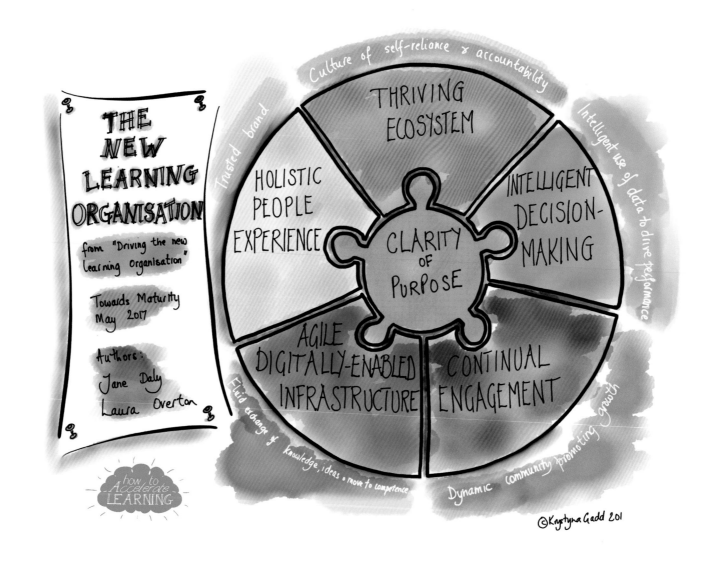

THE NEW LEARNING ORGANISATION

from "Driving the new Learning Organisation"

Towards Maturity May 2017

Authors:
Jane Daly
Laura Overton

how to Accelerate LEARNING

Culture of self-reliance & accountability

Trusted brand

Intelligent use of data to drive performance

THRIVING ECOSYSTEM

HOLISTIC PEOPLE EXPERIENCE

CLARITY OF PURPOSE

INTELLIGENT DECISION-MAKING

AGILE DIGITALLY-ENABLED INFRASTRUCTURE

CONTINUAL ENGAGEMENT

Fluid exchange of knowledge, ideas & move to competence

Dynamic community promoting growth

©Krystyna Gadd 201

104

Frances and Roland Bee in their book *Managing Information and Statistics*[15] talk about one chief reason for managing data and that is for competitive advantage. Using information informs people of:

- The goods or services they should provide
- The differences in what they provide against their competitors
- How the services could be improved.

Bearing these points in mind, I've written on what a new learning leader should be doing to enable an organisation to gain competitive advantage. In my articles for *Training Journal* in 2013[16] and 2016[17] I introduced and then elaborated on the 'five secrets of accelerated learning' (see diagram below), the first secret being business-focussed and learner-centred objectives.

This one is the key, because if your learning interventions are not focussed on the organisation, you will never get the support and resources you need to see them through. And if they are not learner-centred, you will not get buy-in, nor will you see any improvements in the performance the organisation needs.

I believe that L&D's ultimate aim is to help people perform better. That may be through:

- Being clear on what performance improvements are needed for the organisation to achieve its goals
- Going beyond what might present itself as a learning need and digging deeper to find out if it is that or something else (resource requirement, process deficiency, poor communication, etc.)
- Using data to inform good decision-making on where we can help to improve performance through learning
- Curating the materials that the business needs to do this
- Putting together learning materials to support improvements in performance.

In Appendix B, you can reflect on other factors I consider are part of the emerging New Learning Leader role.

So, if our role is to help improve performance, here is what we need to be clear on before collecting data:

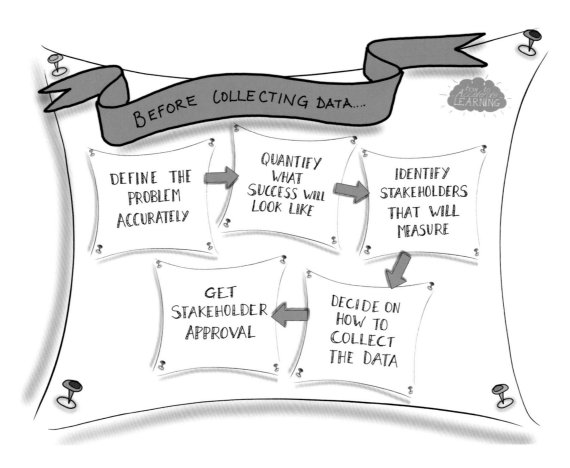

1. Define the problem (Objective 1.2).
2. Define what you are trying to improve in specific, quantifiable terms. For example, "Reduce the number of customer complaints from 18 to 13 per month by the second quarter."
3. Identify the stakeholders that will be measuring this performance improvement (Objective 1.3) and ensure you can do a 'pre-measure' – 'drawing the line in the sand'.
4. Decide on at least three methods of needs analysis (Objective 2.7) and a timeline, as well as resources required. Keep asking yourself, *What information will I get when I use this method (qualitative or quantitative)?*
5. Get approval from the stakeholders to go ahead with the timescales agreed.

When does data become information to feed good decision-making?

Previously,we saw that raw data in itself does not inform our decision-making or improve performance. We have to manipulate or analyse the data to make some sense of it. Let's have a look at how we start to order and analyse data.

Case Study Part 5

This is the next part of the case study, detailing what I did with some of the data collected.

In the table below is some data downloaded from Survey Monkey. The team leaders scored themselves on a scale of 1 to 6, where 1=little or no skill/knowledge and 6=no development needed.

As you look at the table, you may start to see high and low scores, but it is difficult to spot any trends or patterns. This is where a little analysis will start to change the raw data into information that you can use.

The Raw Data

Name	Forward thinking	Inspiring a culture of creativity and innovation	Managing resources	Communicating clearly	Managing the day to day functions of team	Empowering the team	Commitment to company strategy	Driving forward a quality culture	Focusing on results	Managing conflict
John	3	4	5	2	5	4	3	4	5	1
Anthony	4	3	5	4	5	4	5	4	5	4
Brian	5	5	6	5	5	6	5	5	6	5
Peter	5	5	6	4	6	5	5	6	5	4
Andrew	4	6	5	6	5	5	5	6	5	3
Lisa	4	4	5	4	5	4	5	5	5	5
Sophie	5	4	6	3	6	5	5	4	5	4
James	3	4	5	2	5	4	3	4	5	5
Callum	5	5	5	6	6	5	5	4	5	6
Anton	2	3	3	4	4	2	4	4	5	1
Keith	4	2	2	4	4	3	1	3	3	5

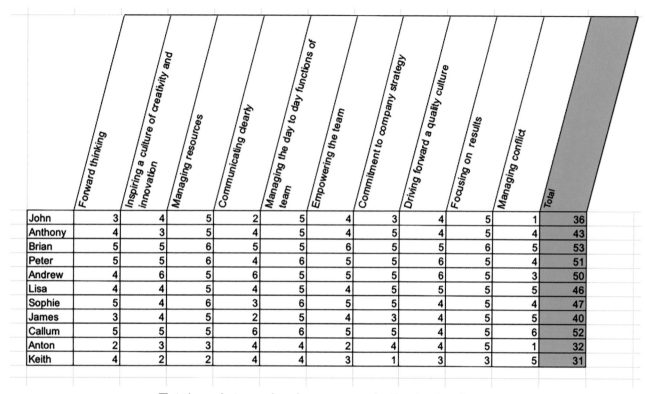

	Forward thinking	Inspiring a culture of creativity and innovation	Managing resources	Communicating clearly	Managing the day to day functions of team	Empowering the team	Commitment to company strategy	Driving forward a quality culture	Focusing on results	Managing conflict	Total
John	3	4	5	2	5	4	3	4	5	1	36
Anthony	4	3	5	4	5	4	5	4	5	4	43
Brian	5	5	6	5	5	6	5	5	6	5	53
Peter	5	5	6	4	6	5	5	6	5	4	51
Andrew	4	6	5	6	5	5	5	6	5	3	50
Lisa	4	4	5	4	5	4	5	5	5	5	46
Sophie	5	4	6	3	6	5	5	4	5	4	47
James	3	4	5	2	5	4	3	4	5	5	40
Callum	5	5	5	6	6	5	5	4	5	6	52
Anton	2	3	3	4	4	2	4	4	5	1	32
Keith	4	2	2	4	4	3	1	3	3	5	31

Total each team leaders scores in the last column

Even this tiny bit of very simple analysis, begins to inform us. We can see what each team leader thinks of themselves in terms of the 10 competencies. Having asked the question of the senior team, "Who are the best team leaders and who are the ones who have least skills?", I had an idea of what the ranking should be if:

- People were honest
- People had a realistic view of their level of skill/knowledge.

One of the people with the lowest skill/levels (as perceived by the SMT) appeared at the top of the self-ranked list, which spoke volumes.

This raised more questions:

- Why do they not know that their skills aren't up to scratch? (Lack of line manager feedback? Lack of intrapersonal skills?)
- If they do know that their skills are not as high as ranked, why are they not being honest? (Blame culture? Job security threat?)

Stage 2

Self scored ranking		Forward thinking	Inspiring a culture of creativity and innovation	Managing resources	Communicating clearly	Managing the day to day functions of team	Empowering the team	Commitment to company strategy	Driving forward a quality culture	Focusing on results	Managing conflict	Total
1	Brian	5	5	6	5	5	6	5	5	6	5	53
2	Callum	5	5	5	6	6	5	5	4	5	6	52
3	Peter	5	5	6	4	6	5	5	6	5	4	51
4	Andrew	4	6	5	6	5	5	5	6	5	3	50
5	Sophie	5	4	6	3	6	5	5	4	5	4	47
6	Lisa	4	4	5	4	5	4	5	5	5	5	46
7	Anthony	4	3	5	4	5	4	5	4	5	4	43
8	James	3	4	5	2	5	4	3	4	5	5	40
9	John	3	4	5	2	5	4	3	4	5	1	36
10	Anton	2	3	3	4	4	2	4	4	5	1	32
11	Keith	4	2	2	4	4	3	1	3	3	5	31

Re-order the list ranking them from highest to lowest (self-ranking scores)

This data analysis has now provided us with some information:

1. Not all the team leaders have realistic views of their level of skill or knowledge
2. The top self-ranked team leader is also the SMT's top-ranked team leader, showing that this person is probably emotionally intelligent, understands what the SMT expects and knows what is expected of him.

Stage 3

In this next stage, I would begin to look at individual scores, highs and lows. The scoring range is from 1 to 6 and so I would look at these scores in this way, using a traffic light analogy:

Scored 5-6: Optimal level of skill/knowledge (green light)
Scored 3-4: Lowest acceptable level of skill/knowledge (amber light)
Scored 1-2: Unacceptable level of skill/knowledge (red light)

Self scored ranking		Forward thinking	Inspiring a culture of creativity and innovation	Managing resources	Communicating clearly	Managing the day to day functions of team	Empowering the team	Commitment to company strategy	Driving forward a quality culture	Focusing on results	Managing conflict	Total
1	Brian	5	5	6	5	5	6	5	5	6	5	53
2	Callum	5	5	5	6	6	5	5	4	5	6	52
3	Peter	5	5	6	4	6	5	5	6	5	4	51
4	Andrew	4	6	5	6	5	5	5	6	5	3	50
5	Sophie	5	4	6	3	6	5	5	4	5	4	47
6	Lisa	4	4	5	4	5	4	5	5	5	5	46
7	Anthony	4	3	5	4	5	4	5	4	5	4	43
8	James	3	4	5	2	5	4	3	4	5	5	40
9	John	3	4	5	2	5	4	3	4	5	1	36
10	Anton	2	3	3	4	4	2	4	4	5	1	32
11	Keith	4	2	2	4	4	3	1	3	3	5	31

1-2
3-4
5-6

Using this colour-coding allows you to see easily where the hotspots are: who has the most 'red light' or 'green light' areas. You can also see which of the competencies will need most attention.

Remember, this is just how they scored themselves, which is not necessarily a true and accurate picture. It is part of the story that is emerging. That is why you need more than one data source to confirm what you believe may be true. This is where the opinions of the senior managers help to put things in perspective as well as give some insights into the relationships between the team leaders and their senior managers.

A question I inserted into the questionnaire as a 'hunch' turned out to be helpful in shedding light on the relationships between the team leaders and their senior manager.

6. How much support do you get from your line manager?

- Too much

- Sometimes too much

- Just about right

- Sometimes not enough

- Not enough

The team leader who appeared at the bottom of the ranking chose the option 'not enough' and left a comment to say he also felt 'overlooked and unsupported'. Four out of those who responded to this question said they did not spend enough time with their senior manager. As a result, I included in the programme opportunities for the team leaders and their senior team to meet before each workshop to:

- Reflect on the previous workshop, and state what went well and what they needed to put into action
- Set objectives and reflect on what they wanted to get out of the next workshop and what their senior manager felt they needed to focus on.

In this table are perceptions of the team leaders on how they score against the competencies. They will give you an idea of how confident (rightly or wrongly) they might be in each area. One of the reasons they may not be realistic in their estimation of how good they are may be where they fall on the Conscious Competence (diagram) grid.

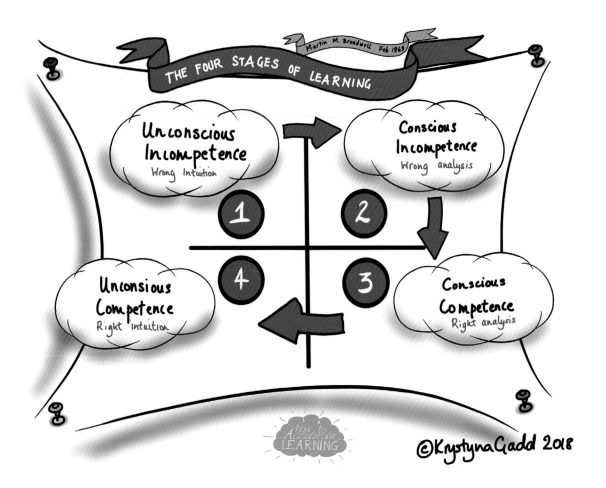

Interestingly, not everyone who attended completed the survey, which in itself may allow us to draw some conclusions about the type of culture present:

- Blame culture?
- Fear culture?

Stage 4

Self scored ranking		Forward thinking	Inspiring a culture of creativity and innovation	Managing resources	Communicating clearly	Managing the day to day functions of team	Empowering the team	Commitment to company strategy	Driving forward a quality culture	Focusing on results	Managing conflict	Total
1	Brian	5	5	6	5	5	6	5	5	6	5	53
2	Callum	5	5	5	6	6	5	5	4	5	6	52
3	Peter	5	5	6	4	6	5	5	6	5	4	51
4	Andrew	4	6	5	6	5	5	5	6	5	3	50
5	Sophie	5	4	6	3	6	5	5	4	5	4	47
6	Lisa	4	4	5	4	5	4	5	5	5	5	46
7	Anthony	4	3	5	4	5	4	5	4	5	4	43
8	James	3	4	5	2	5	4	3	4	5	5	40
9	John	3	4	5	2	5	4	3	4	5	1	36
10	Anton	2	3	3	4	4	2	4	4	5	1	32
11	Keith	4	2	2	4	4	3	1	3	3	5	31
		44	45	53	44	56	47	46	49	54	43 out of 60	

1-2
3-4
5-6

Total up the scores for each competency to see which is the lowest scoring and which the highest scoring

From the table below, you can see that 'managing conflict' was the lowest scoring of the competencies and 'managing the day-to-day functions of the team' was the highest. This fits in with what the SMT anecdotally shared in their half-day session. They mentioned that the team leaders 'constantly' came to them to resolve conflict in their teams. They also shared that they felt the team leaders needed to develop their leadership skills as opposed to their management skills.

Stage 5

Once I had ordered the self-scored competencies of the team leaders, I was curious to see how these compared to how the SMT ranked the importance of the competencies. As you can see from the table, the two are almost in opposite orders.

Self scored ranking		Forward thinking	Inspiring a culture of creativity and innovation	Managing resources	Communicating clearly	Managing the day to day functions of team	Empowering the team	Commitment to company strategy	Driving forward a quality culture	Focusing on results	Managing conflict	Total
1	Brian	5	5	6	5	5	6	5	5	6	5	53
2	Callum	5	5	5	6	6	5	5	4	5	6	52
3	Peter	5	5	6	4	6	5	5	6	5	4	51
4	Andrew	4	6	5	6	5	5	5	6	5	3	50
5	Sophie	5	4	6	3	6	5	5	4	5	4	47
6	Lisa	4	4	5	4	5	4	5	5	5	5	46
7	Anthony	4	3	5	4	5	4	5	4	5	4	43
8	James	3	4	5	2	5	4	3	4	5	5	40
9	John	3	4	5	2	5	4	3	4	5	1	36
10	Anton	2	3	3	4	4	2	4	4	5	1	32
11	Keith	4	2	2	4	4	3	1	3	3	5	31
		44	45	53	44	56	47	46	49	54	43	out of 60
		8	7	3	8	1	5	6	4	2	10	rank
		2	6	8	3	10	4	7	5	9	1	SMT rank of importance

1-2
3-4
5-6

To visualise this, I used a line graph.

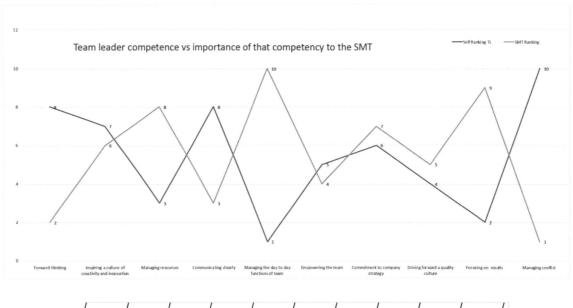

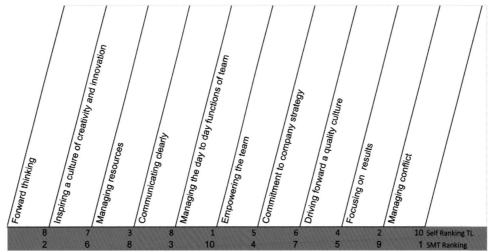

	Forward thinking	Inspiring a culture of creativity and innovation	Managing resources	Communicating clearly	Managing the day to day functions of team	Empowering the team	Commitment to company strategy	Driving forward a quality culture	Focusing on results	Managing conflict	
	8	7	3	8	1	5	6	4	2	10	Self Ranking TL
	2	6	8	3	10	4	7	5	9	1	SMT Ranking

117

This graph comes directly from the data in the table above. In this format it is hard to see what is going on until you order the competencies in order of their ranking and then it is in the second graph that the story starts to emerge.

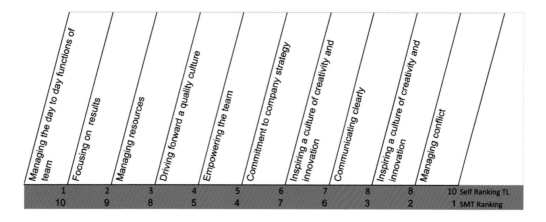

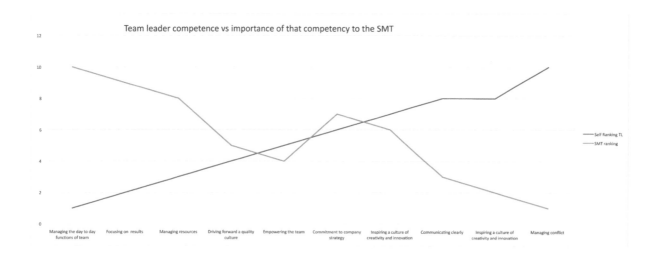

In this line graph, you can see clearly that the areas most important to the SMT are the ones where the team leaders score lowest and vice versa.

It now becomes useful to know how to present the data so that the patterns you have spotted (or not yet spotted) are evident to any reader. Sometimes it is only when you have taken the data and placed it into a graph or chart that the pattern emerges. We will cover this in the next section.

Objective 3.8

Create an action plan for what you are going to do before you begin collecting data.

In this chapter, you have had an opportunity to see how your gut feel can help or hinder you in your approach to collecting data. You have also seen the connection between collecting raw data and performance improvement. Through the case study, you have seen how easy it is to see the story emerge from the numbers. Hopefully, from this step-by-step demonstration, you appreciate how simple a needs analysis can be. Surely, it is better to do something simple than nothing at all.

Now for a quick recap of what you have covered in this chapter and what you should be able to do:

Objectives:

3.1 Differentiate between the gut feelings you have experienced in past decisions you have made and the more analytical approach.

Completed (date and sign)...

3.2 Describe why it is important to collect data.

Completed (date and sign)...

3.3 Relate what you do to what the organisational goals are.

Completed (date and sign)...

3.4 Define some key measures for your role in line with organisational requirements.

Completed (date and sign)...

3.5 Differentiate between data and information.

Completed (date and sign)...

3.6 Differentiate between qualitative and quantitative data.

Completed (date and sign)...

Objectives:

3.7 For three case studies, choose the format the data will take.

Completed (date and sign)...

3.8 Describe what you need to do before you start collecting your data.

Completed (date and sign)...

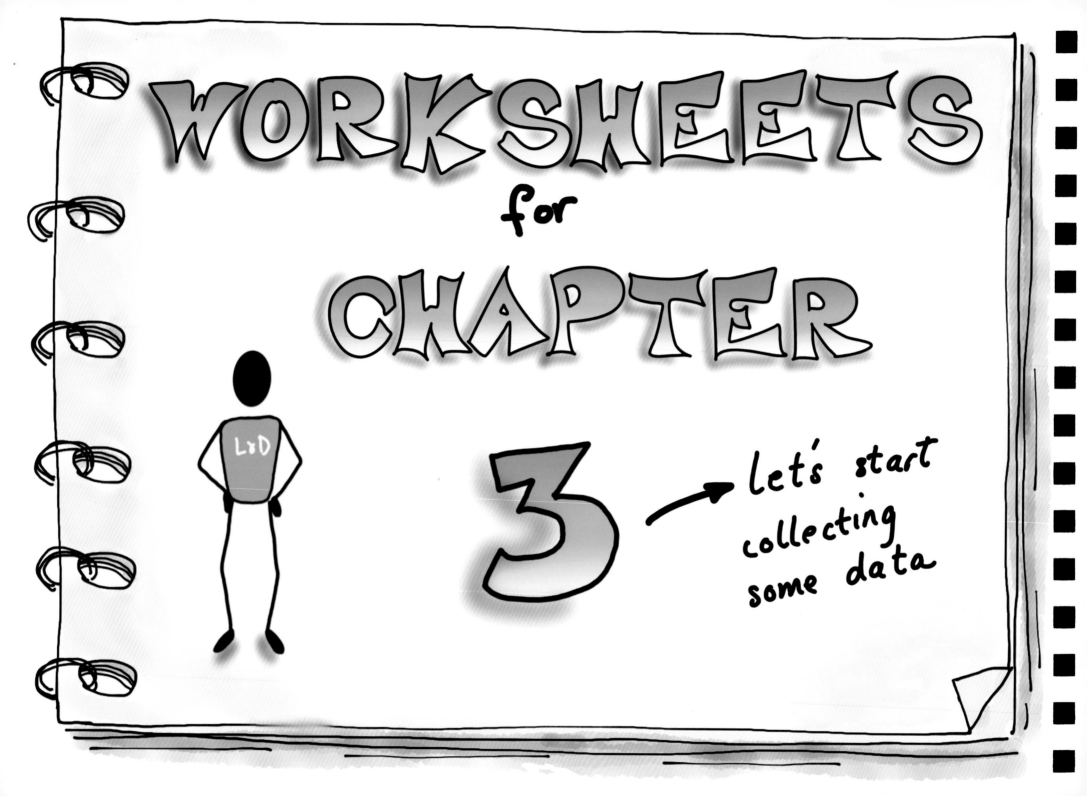

3.1 Developing your decision making skills

©KrystynaGadd 201

WHY WE SHOULD COLLECT DATA

How will my team and my manager benefit?

How will I benefit?

How will the organisation benefit?

©Krystyna Gadd 2018

124

3.3 3.4 Relating what you do to organisational goals

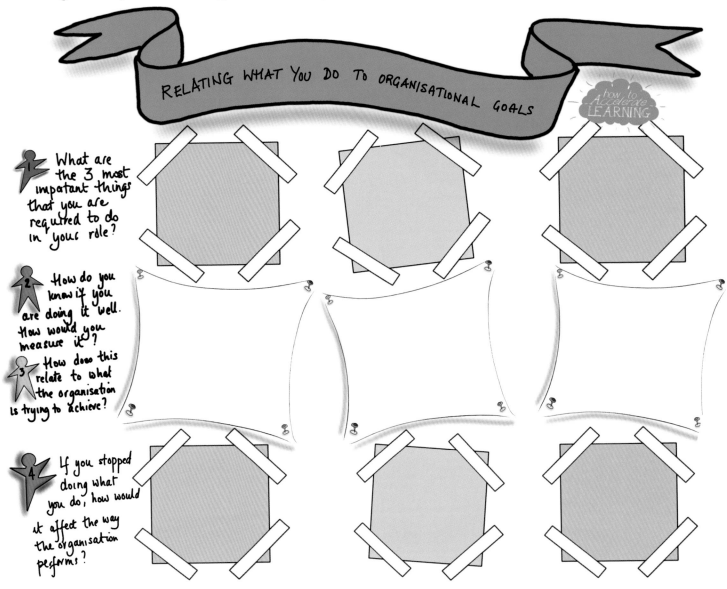

RELATING WHAT YOU DO TO ORGANISATIONAL GOALS

how to Accelerate LEARNING

1 What are the 3 most important things that you are required to do in your role?

2 How do you know if you are doing it well. How would you measure it?

3 How does this relate to what the organisation is trying to achieve?

4 If you stopped doing what you do, how would it affect the way the organisation performs?

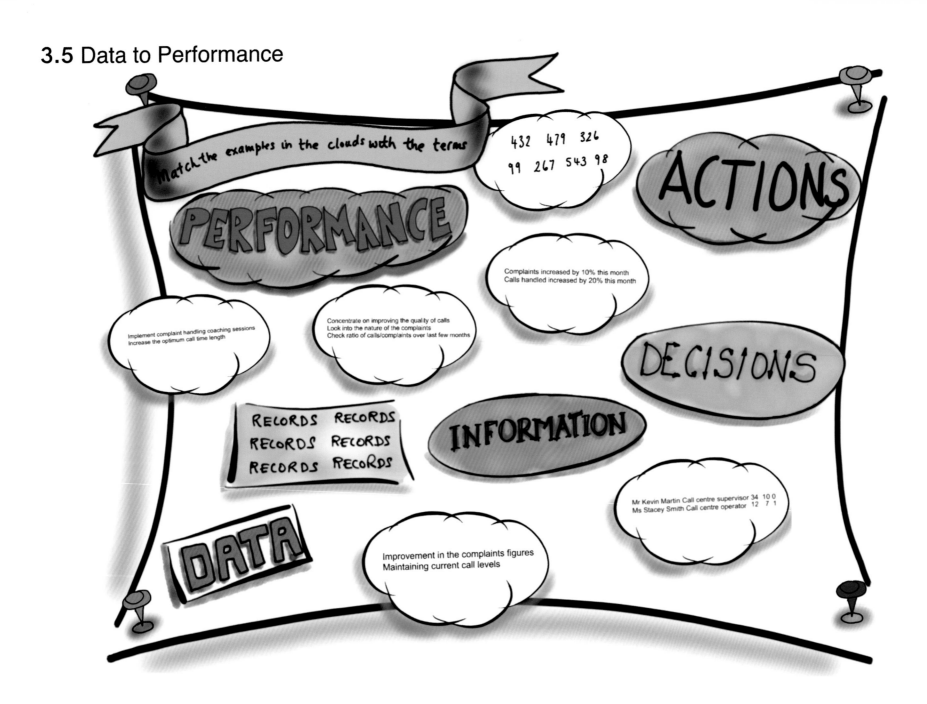

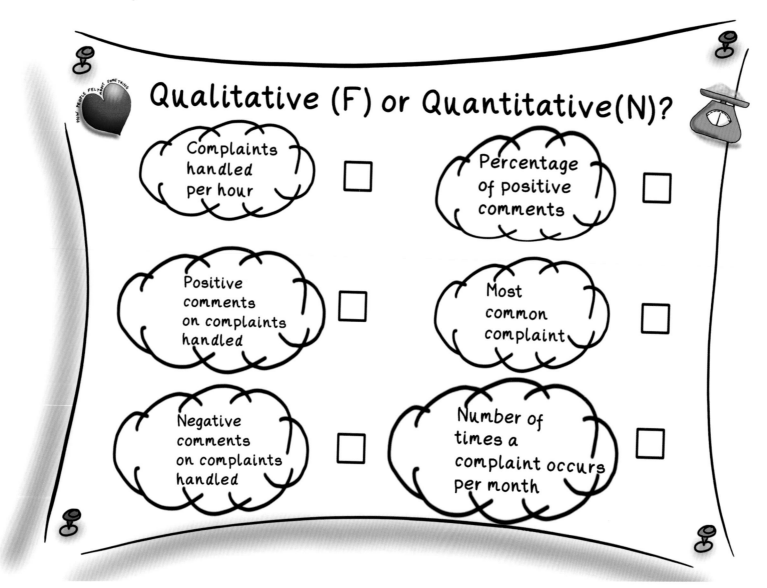

Qualitative (F) or Quantitative(N)?

- Complaints handled per hour ☐
- Percentage of positive comments ☐
- Positive comments on complaints handled ☐
- Most common complaint ☐
- Negative comments on complaints handled ☐
- Number of times a complaint occurs per month ☐

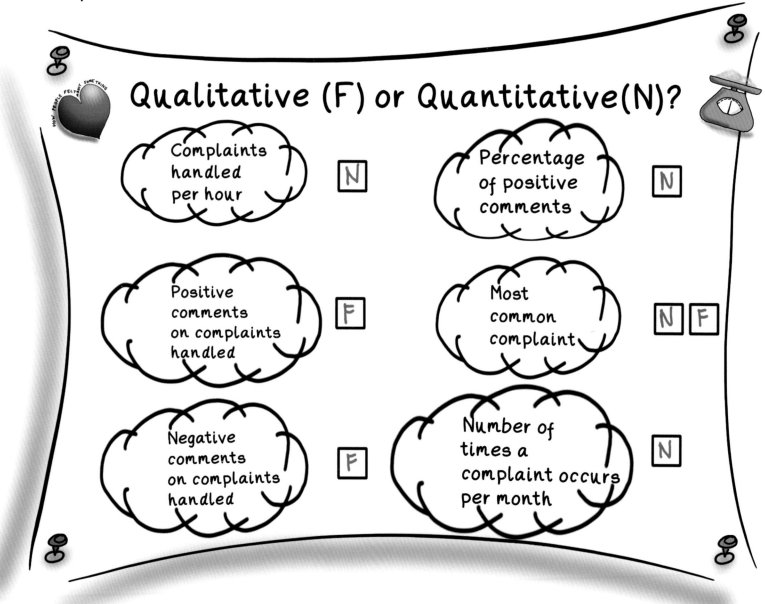

Qualitative (F) or Quantitative(N)?

Complaints handled per hour — N

Percentage of positive comments — N

Positive comments on complaints handled — F

Most common complaint — N F

Negative comments on complaints handled — F

Number of times a complaint occurs per month — N

3.7 LNA Case Studies

For the case studies from 2.5 describe what form the data will take

1. Customer complaints begin to rise in the customer service team as a whole and no one seems to know the real cause. Some people, though not all, have been struggling with some of the online tools. How would you begin an analysis to uncover what is going on behind the scenes? Which methods would you choose?

	Name of method	Format of the data
LNA Method 1		
LNA Method 2		
LNA Method 3		

2. A new team member arrives, who you know has not got all the relevant experience required but has a great "can-do" attitude and a real willingness to learn. How could you get an accurate picture of what they need to learn to get to speed quickly?

	Name of method	Format of the data
LNA Method 1		
LNA Method 2		
LNA Method 3		

3. Your organisation is about to move into new markets by buying out an existing company. Most of the staff will be kept on and you have plans to expand the market share, so will need some of your staff to gain new skills in this area. You will probably need to recruit more staff too in order to serve the geographical areas you wish to cover.

	Name of method	Format of the data
LNA Method 1		
LNA Method 2		
LNA Method 3		

3.7 LNA Case Studies Answers

This activity will help you think before choosing a learning method or indeed an analysis method for determining the learning needs of your teams.

For each of these scenarios, consider, how you might dig deeper and which methods you might use to do a thorough analysis. Consider not only the people involved, but those affected by the things that are going on.

1. Customer complaints begin to rise in the team as a whole and no one seems to know the real cause. Some people, though not all, have been struggling with some of the online tools. How would you begin an analysis to uncover what is going on behind the scenes? Which methods would you choose?
   - *Gather all figures over a number of months detailing the customer complaints summed up for the team and also individuals – analyse in a spreadsheet showing how each team member is performing. If the performance is consistently declining for everyone then the following methods apply to everyone. If not, then just target the individuals concerned.*
   - *Gather customers comments to see if there are any clues as to what may be going wrong*
   - *Interview individuals or create a focus group from your team to dig deeper into the casues.*

2. A new team member arrives, who you know has not got all the relevant experience required, but has a great "can-do" attitude and a real willingness to learn. How could you get an accurate picture of what they need to learn to get to speed quickly?
   - *Job analysis using their job description and their CV*
   - *Use the output from above to interview the new team member to get their thoughts about what they need*
   - *Buddy up with a peer to observe the actual performance of the new starter*

3. There has been some conflict in your team and also some of your targets have not been met. A couple of people are on performance improvement plans, but there are mutterings that the right people have not been targeted. How would you start to

analyse what is going on and which methods could you use to get an accurate picture of what is going on (or not going on).

- *360 feedback tool to get feedback on all the team. If there are mutterings you must approach this in a fair and systematic way; not being swayed by the mutterings but not ignoring that there is conflict occurring*
- *Check the measures you have in place to identify poor performers*
- *Based on the output above, interview those that get poor feedback on their performance and that you can identify from any departmental measures, plus those that are muttering about the wrong people being targetted*

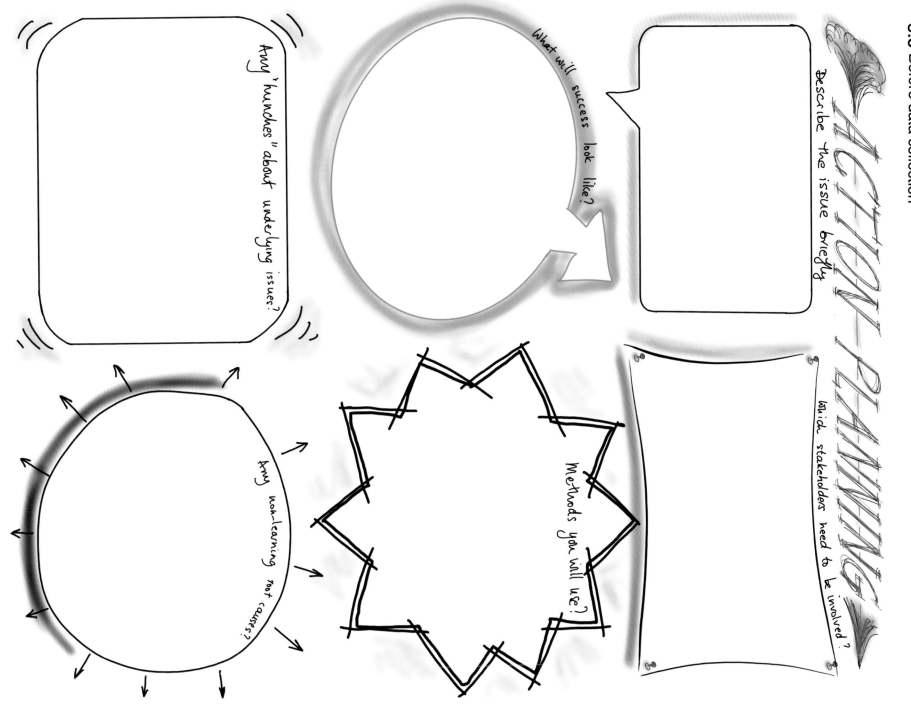

ACTION-PLANNING

Describe the issue briefly

What will success look like?

Any "hunches" about underlying issues?

Which stakeholders need to be involved?

Methods you will use?

Any non-learning root causes?

Finding the story in the numbers

Objectives:

By the end of the chapter, you will be able to:

4.1 Select an appropriate method for visually presenting a set of data.
4.2 Describe how to draw conclusions from the data.
4.3 List some of the limitations of the data/chart that you are using.
4.4 Identify any bias that you may have in relation to the data you are collecting.
4.5 Differentiate between aims, organisational objectives, performance objectives and learning outcomes (objectives).
4.6 Set some clear organisational objectives for a set of outcomes.
4.7 Identify correctly the learning levels required according to Bloom's Taxonomy.
4.8 Set some specific performance objectives for given examples.
4.9 Devise some learning outcomes for a given case study using Robert Mager's PCS framework.

At this stage of the analysis, it is important that you do not lose sight of what you are trying to do. In Chapter 1, I mentioned the purpose of L&D:

The whole purpose of L&D is not to design and deliver learning, but to help the business improve its performance. [...] At times, it may be through identifying gaps that can be filled with learning. At other times, it may be that you have done a little digging and found something other than lack of learning to be the cause of a performance issue. It is important that we know the difference.

Looking at the data, are you beginning to see the story emerge? The story of 'why performance is flagging in this area'?

In the last part of the case study, I mentioned how I had a hunch that the lack of clarity or honesty about team leaders' own competencies was due to insufficient time being spent with their own senior managers. This starts to go beyond just a learning need and emphasises how important the role of L&D is in identifying 'something missing' that is causing a performance issue. Due to the overarching nature of the L&D function, we are in a unique position to observe relationships, interrelationships and friction, where others might not.

Presenting and using the data to inform

The graph below clearly shows an orange line where the competencies are ranked in order of decreasing importance (1 being the most important and 10 the least)

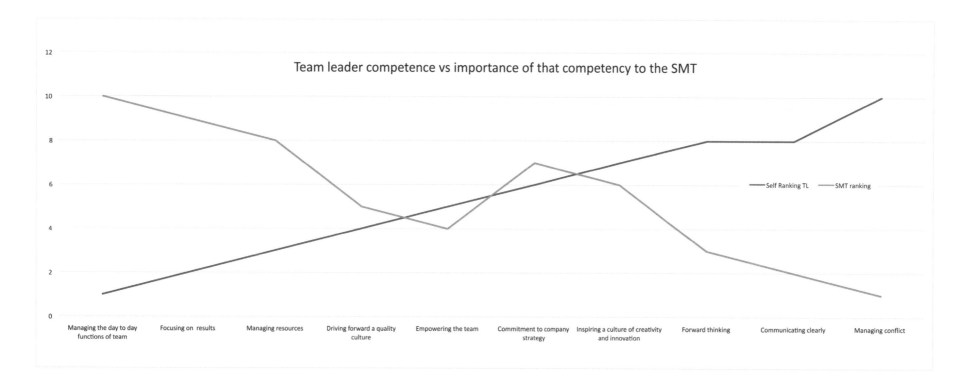

Importance increases by an upward sloping line. In the above graph, the orange line indicates the importance of the competencies as viewed by the senior managers. So managing conflict is the most important and managing the day-to-day functions is the least important.

Let's make this clearer:

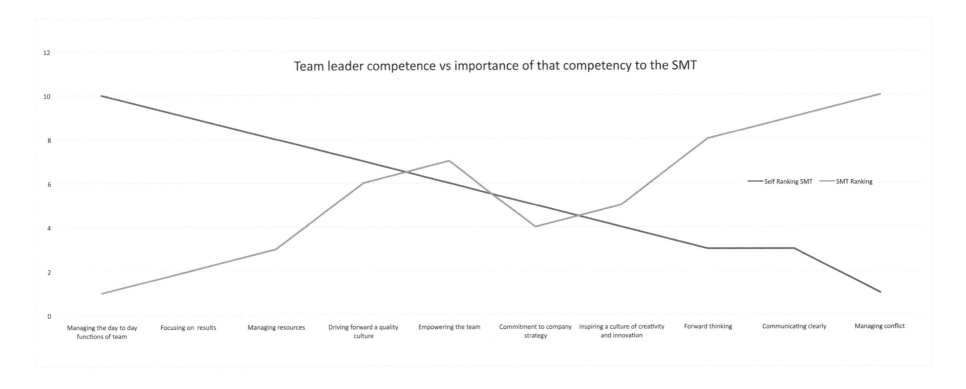

In this version, we can see there is a progression for the self-ranking scores from the team leaders that 'conflict management' is less important than 'managing the day-to-day'. The chart is telling us a clear story: the team leaders score themselves such that it is the opposite to what the SMT feels they need. If you were presenting this in a report or a presentation, it would be easy to see and interpret. The message is evident.

Sometimes you just have to play around with a graph before it is feels right and becomes crystal clear. If you are not sure, get some feedback on it from someone else and ask if they can tell you what the graph is saying without your explaining.

Selecting the most appropriate chart or graph format

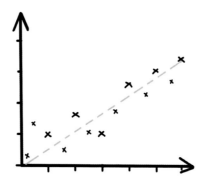 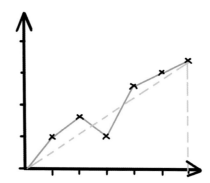

This is a simple scatter diagram. A lot of data has been collected and this shows the relationship of the data collected to an average line. It can help to show the variety of the data and how far it strays from the overall average.

If the data follows an average line more closely, then a simple line diagram may work better than a scatter diagram. The line may not be a straight one, but it will show the relationship that the data follows. You can join the points as well as superimpose the nearest approximation to a line the data takes.

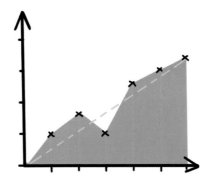 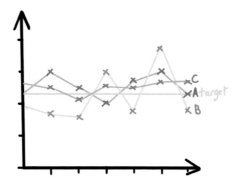

A variation of the previous chart is showing the area underneath the line that the data occupies. For more than one data line, where values are not similar, the differences can be seen easily using a different colour.

This is another variation of the chart above, showing different data sets and their relationship to an average. The data sets could be for different people, months or years. Where the previous chart shows how different the data sets are, this one could more readily show similarities.

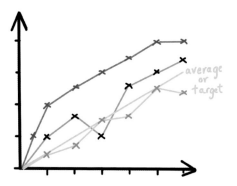

The chart to the left is another variation of the previous, showing a trend in data sets and their relationship to a target or average.

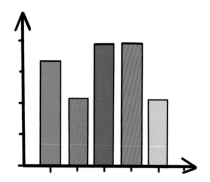

A bar chart for a single data set shows clearly how something varies with time, by month, person or other category. A variation of this could be having bars of the same colour for several years compared to each other.

This is another variety of a bar chart, called a stacked bar. Within each data set, there may be further detail and so this chart shows how each bar is composed.

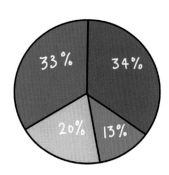

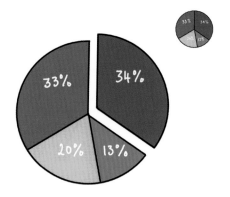

A simple pie chart shows percentages or portions of a whole in a visual way. The data has to be expressed in percentages to create the graph.

In order to emphasise a part of the data, you can use this 'exploded pie chart'.

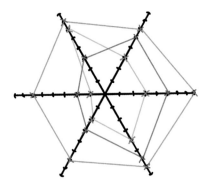

Whereas a line graph shows the relationship between one thing (like time) and another thing (like sales figures), a spider diagram has more than two axes (this one has six). For example, one data set (in one colour) could be measuring six different things, like competencies in a particular role.

Look at the data below and options for displaying the information graphically. This uses the concept of a scoring grid, comparing several people in their roles against each other to determine what the gaps in knowledge, skills or behaviour may be. The roles are the same, but the competency of each individual will be different. This example is a customer service role and all the scores are out of 10 (1 = not very proficient, 10 = expert).

	Product Knowledge	Systems Knowledge	Call-handling skills	Objection-handling skills	Sales skills	Works independently on initiative
Tracy	8	7	8	7	9	9
Martin	5	6	7	8	8	6
Andy	4	8	8	9	9	5
Colin	7	8	6	6	5	8
Sheila	9	8	9	8	8	4

Some options:

1. **Column or bar chart with multiple data sets** – one for each member of the team

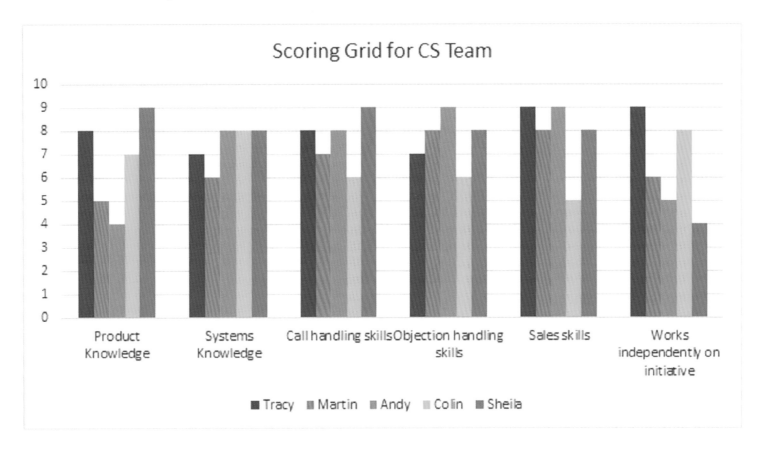

What it tells you: Good comparison one person against another for each part of their role.

What it does not tell you: As a team, how are they doing as a whole? What are the weakest aspects of their role overall? Which person is the strongest? Which person is the weakest?

2. **Spider diagram**

What it tells you: Shows how well-rounded each team member is in their own right. Some are not rounded at all! Tracy seems the most well-rounded.

What it does not tell you: Where or who you should concentrate any development on. Not very easy to decipher averages.

3. **Stacked column/bar chart** – stacked per aspect of their role

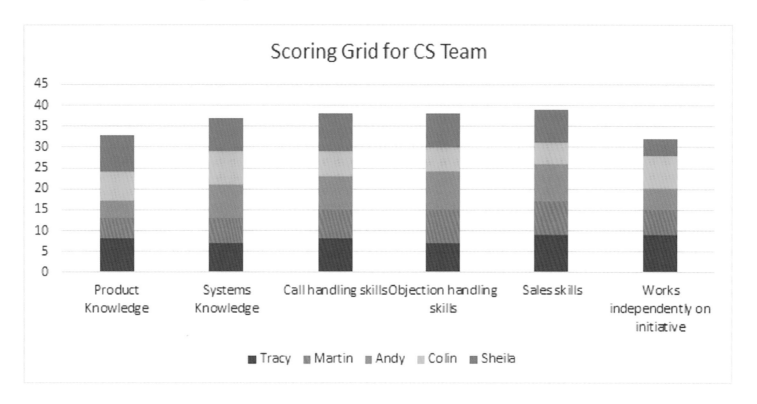

What it tells you: Shows the team's strengths and weaknesses

- Strongest in 'sales skills'
- Weakest in 'product knowledge' and 'working independently'

You can then consider why this might be. Could the manager be poor at delegating, for example?

What it does not tell you: Which individual is the strongest or weakest.

4. **Stacked column/bar chart** – stacked per person

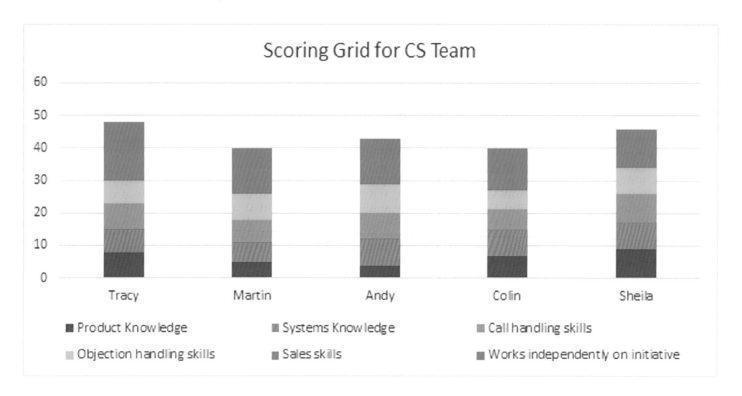

What it tells you: This is great for showing the strongest and weakest team members. Tracy and Sheila are the strongest while Martin and Colin are the weakest.

What it does not tell you: Team weaknesses and strengths in aspects of their role.

ACTIVITY

Objective 4.1, 4.2 and 4.3

Put together a simple spreadsheet using some real data – maybe from your own team. Start with some simple data you have collected and think about three different ways that you can present the data. Consider how you might draw conclusions from this type of graph and also what limitations there might be on this method.

Data doesn't lie?

It is easy to think that if you are being 'scientific' about needs analysis, then it must be true. Just like our eyes can be fooled into thinking that the picture is either a duck or rabbit, our brains can be fooled by the spin you put on the data. We are all subject to bias, but it's important to know that you are not projecting any undisclosed bias onto the data. Here are some types of bias you may be inflicting on your analysis:

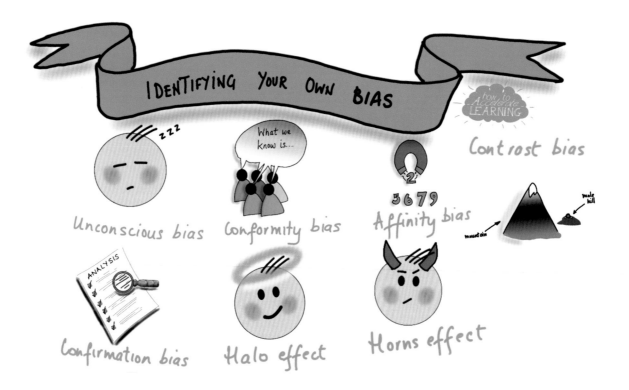

Unconscious bias	Where we make up our minds very quickly about something without thinking too much.
Conformity bias	We follow the 'group thinking' on this by following others' lead on what the data is saying.
Affinity bias	What we are drawn to, we find and confirm.
Confirmation bias	Our initial 'suspicions' are confirmed as soon as the data looks to be confirming what we thought.
Halo effect	If this is true, it will have a huge perceived value and we want to believe it.
Horns effect	The opposite of the above and so we do not want to believe it.
Contrast bias	Mentally upgrading or downgrading something when we compare it to something different.

If something is emerging from the data, is unusual or looks like it is confirming something we already know, question it. Does it make sense? Does anything else confirm this? Be aware of your own feelings about what you are investigating and how bias may be creeping in.

ACTIVITY

Objective 4.4

Consider the different biases and whether you may have a bias in the situation you are dealing with. Be honest with yourself. Use the questions in the worksheet to identify any biases you may have towards the subject you are analysing. Being aware of them may be just what you need to avoid the analysis being skewed.

Setting objectives

152

There is a process you can follow to determine objectives (including the above, which I use). Having looked at some data and decided what the gaps are, the next step will be to see which aspect or aspects of performance you will be targeting.

In the customer sales team example, the weakest areas are 'product knowledge' and 'working independently on initiative'. Before you can set learning outcomes, you need to know what impact on the organisation, if any, you are expecting. You may know this already because it was part of the original brief. I'm sure we've all heard something along the lines of "we're getting too many complaints from customers!"

The graph on the next page shows areas that are weaknesses. Alongside it, I would have other information, for example:

- The number of complaints and the nature of these complaints. (Were they to do with lack of product knowledge?)
- The time it takes to resolve the complaints. (If it takes a long time, it may be because they cannot work independently and have to go to their supervisor or line manager for advice.)
- What is the effect of them not being able to work independently on the job they do and their performance? On their targets? On their team leader?

It may be worthwhile, especially as it is only a small team, to look a little deeper into the issue around not being able to 'work independently on initiative'. At this stage, you may have some suspicions:

- The line manager does not instil confidence in the team by giving affirming and adjusting feedback regularly. If this is the case, then this problem will not be solved by training the team only. It looks like the line manager may need a learning intervention also.
- The lack of product knowledge is causing a lack of confidence – this may be the case for Andy but not Sheila, who has a good product knowledge. Her lack of being able to work on her own initiative may be due to other factors, so far unseen (such as absence, poor relationship with manager or co-workers).
- Something else?

Looking at the graph below, we can also identify who is the weakest and who is the strongest in the team. This may help you decide what the best solutions may be for the team and individuals.

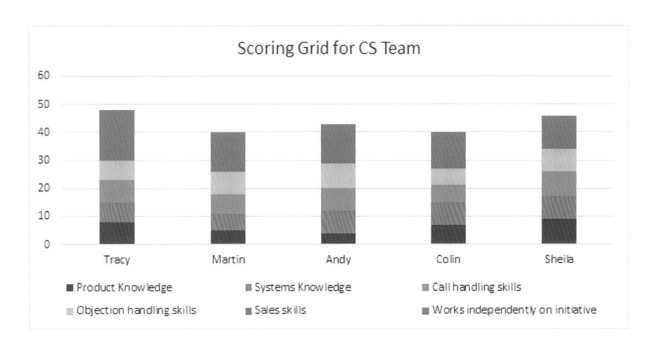

Let's get back to the objectives.

If the product knowledge improved, might that:

- Increase sales?
- Decrease complaints?

If they were all able to work independently on their own initiative, it is likely that the same two metrics would be applicable. In addition, it may improve the customer or employee experience. In turn, that may affect the attrition rate of the team (if, indeed, that is a particular problem).

We need to set clear measurable objectives to see performance improvements and not woolly aims. If you are in any doubt what the difference between aims and other types of objectives are then see the two diagrams below.

155

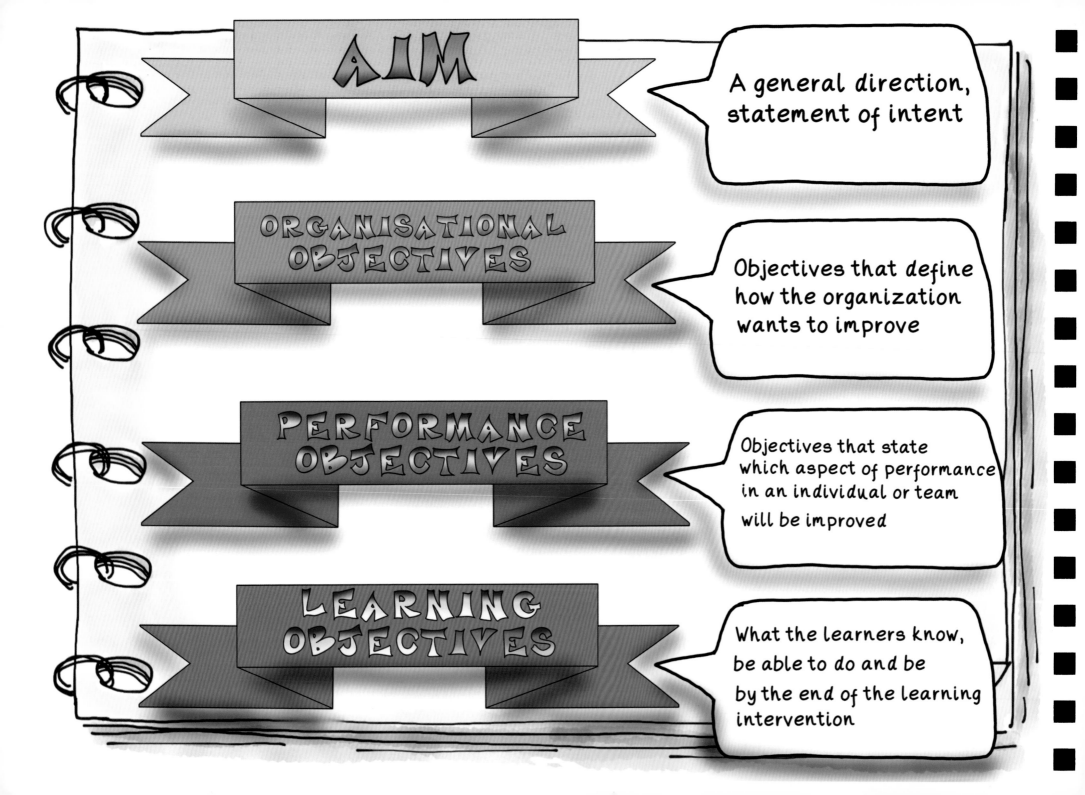

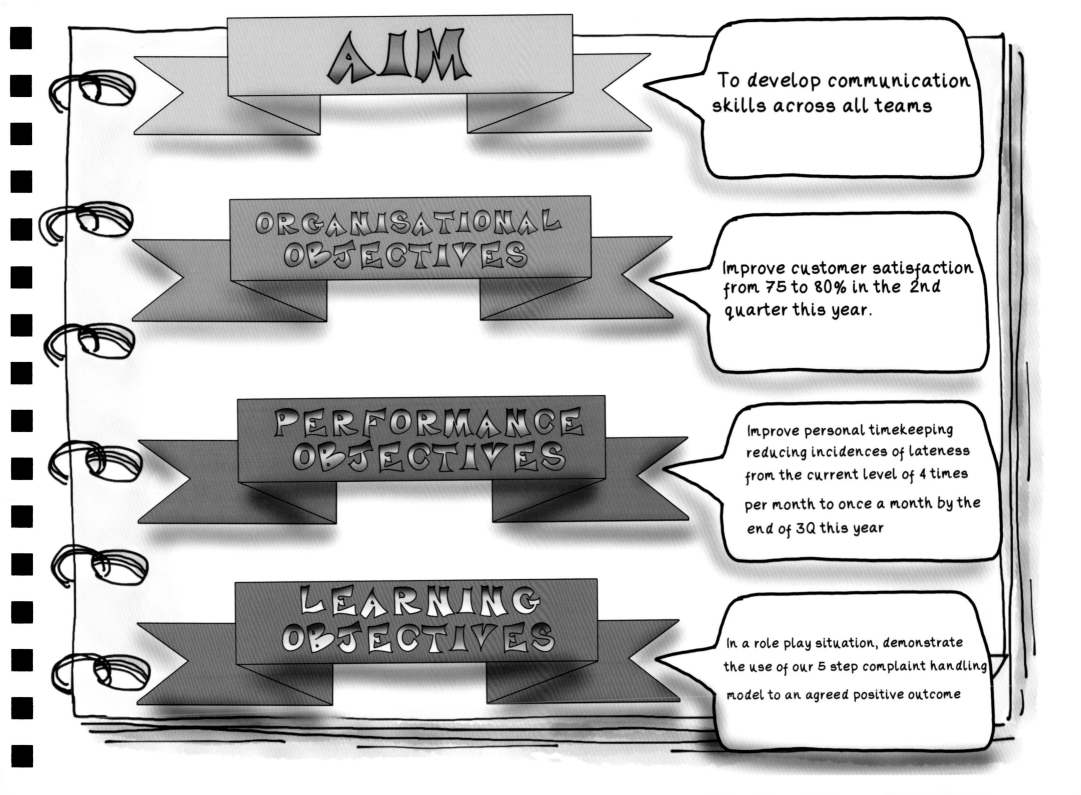

Having identified some issues, there are some potential remedies that could be put in place. It depends on why the needs analysis was conducted in the first place.

Keeping it simple, let's assume what needs to happen is:

> "The customer experience needs to improve."

This can be classed as an aim, as it is vague, woolly and difficult to measure. It is, however, useful as a guide towards reaching some achievable outcomes. Some of the specific measures that need to be improved by the organisation are:

> "To reduce the number of complaints from 45 to 30 per month by 3Q.
> To achieve an overall customer satisfaction score of 85% from 76% by 3Q."

These are the organisational outcomes, which it does not take much effort to turn into performance objectives for a team or individual:

> "To reduce the number of complaints per week from 3 to 1 by 3Q.
> To achieve a customer satisfaction score of 88% from 80% by 3Q.
> To resolve 9/10 complaints without needing to escalate to a supervisor by 3Q."

If product knowledge and not being able to work independently on initiative are the main barriers to performance, then reasonable learning outcomes would be:

> 1. "Individually, in a role play and without reference to notes, be able to describe all the key aspects of our main products.
> 2. Individually, with reference to notes, identify the key areas of your customer interactions on your job description, where you feel your confidence is below average.
> 3. Individually, using an action plan, describe what you need to do to improve your confidence in the areas listed in 2."

ACTIVITY

Objective 4.5

Looking at the worksheet examples, can you identify the aims, organisational objectives, performance objectives and learning objectives (outcomes)?

ACTIVITY

Objective 4.6

Create some organisational outcomes from the examples given.

Using Robert Mager's PCS Framework[21]

This is a fabulous framework to create objectives that are easily measured:

The framework has only has three parts and is simple. Once you have decided if it is a knowledge, skills or behaviour issue, you can begin by choosing the right verb to describe the PERFORMANCE part: what it is that you want them to be able to do by the end of the learning intervention. See the table on the next page.

SKILLS					
MENTAL (to do with ideas)		*PHYSICAL* (to do with things)		*PERSONAL* (to do with people)	
Analyse	Modify	Apply	Examine	Advise	Facilitate
Audit	Organise	Adjust	File	Appraise	Manage
Budget	Predict	Align	Fix	Coordinate	Mediate
Catalogue	Prescribe	Arrange	Install	Counsel	Negotiate
Classify	Program	Assemble	Manipulate	Decide	Persuade
Describe	Proofread	Build	Modify	Defend	Resolve
Design	Report	Conduct	Perform	Guide	Supervise
Develop	Research	Connect	Prepare		
Estimate	Revise	Construct	Remove		
Evaluate	Schedule	Complete	Repair		
Forecast	State	Demonstrate	Replace		
Justify	Verify	Detach	Time		
KNOWLEDGE			**ATTITUDES**		
Categorise	Label		Adopt	Demonstrate	
Compare	List		Advocate	Detect	
Define	Name		Appraise	Discriminate	
Depict	Outline		Challenge	Devote	
Describe	Prepare		Choose	Emphasise	
Explain	Recite		Commit	Endorse	
Express	Recount		Contrast	Justify	
Interpret	Relate		Criticise	Practice	
Itemise	Select		Defend	Select	
	Specify				

161

If you are unsure about the level of performance required, then Bloom's Taxonomy can help. Below is a diagram of the three domains.

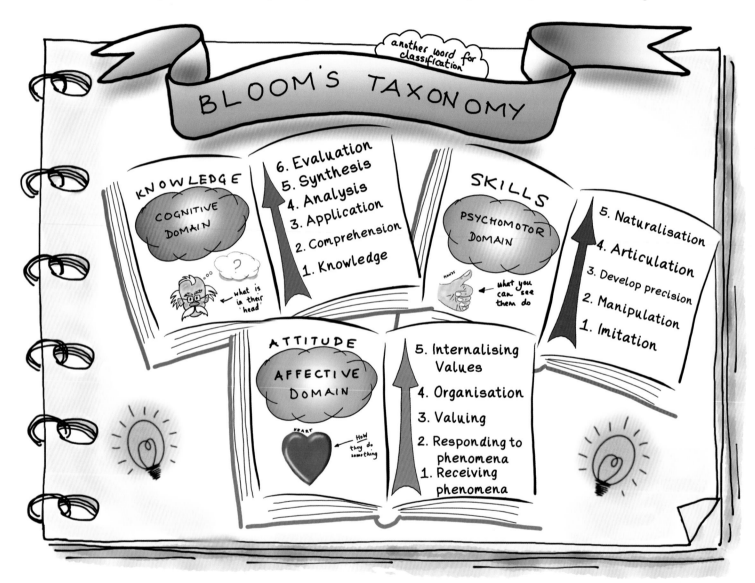

Below are some examples to clarify the levels and the three domains.

ACTIVITY

Objective 4.7

For the case studies below, determine the domain of Bloom's Taxonomy and level of learning.

Conditions

This part of the framework offers us an opportunity to decide under what CONDITIONS they should be able to perform. Remember, this is not back in their role, because you will not be able to observe them. This is during the learning intervention and could be formal or informal (by observation or some type of test, for example).

Here are some conditions:

- Individually (when it is key they can do so)
- In a role play
- Using a case study
- In a group discussion
- With the use of notes
- Without the use of notes

The STANDARD tells us how well you want them to be able to perform. Sometimes it may simply be 'correctly', if the answers are obvious. Other times, the standard may be measured against a well-defined model or an internal framework that you might use.

Here are some standards:

- Following our 5-step customer service model
- Giving at least 5 examples
- Using the AID feedback model

Once you start using this framework, you will see how easy it becomes to not only write strong (SMART) objectives, but to design learning.

Objectives 4.8 and 4.9

In this activity, you will be determining if the sample objectives conform to Robert Mager's PCS Framework. Look at the objectives and check if each has a 'P', 'C' or 'S' component.

At this point, it is worthwhile mentioning and referring to this visual that we saw in Chapter 3. Collecting data in itself is not what this book is about. This book is about improving performance through collecting data and turning it into meaningful information. Once you have good information about what is (or is not) going on in your organisation, you can make informed decisions, set clear objectives for yourself and your people, and see those objectives played out into actions that drive improved performance. If we know what we are looking for in the performance improvements, it means that there will be something for the stakeholders to measure.

And ultimately, that means demonstrating the value you bring easily and straightforwardly.

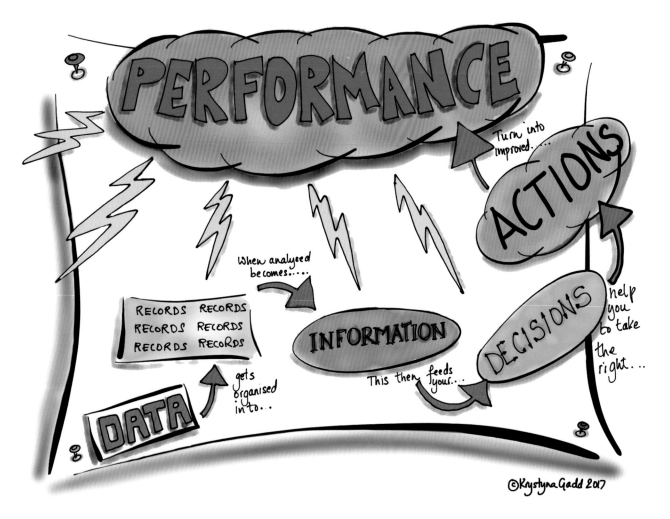

In this chapter, you have seen how to draw conclusions from data as well as choose appropriate ways to present it. In presenting that data, you may introduce a bias, which you are hopefully better at spotting now. And finally, linking learning and performance can only be done if you can set some good objectives.

If this is the first time you have been through this process, I hope it encourages you to seek and analyse data further to verify if learning has had an impact. Take time to reflect on this journey.

Now a quick recap of what you have covered in this chapter and what you should be able to do:

Objectives:

4.1 Select an appropriate method for visually presenting a set of data.

Completed (date and sign)……………………………………………………………

4.2 Describe how to draw conclusions from the data.

Completed (date and sign)……………………………………………………………

4.3 List some of the limitations of the data/chart that you are using.

Completed (date and sign)……………………………………………………………

4.4 Identify any bias that you may have in relation to the data you are collecting.

Completed (date and sign)……………………………………………………………

Objectives:

4.5 Differentiate between aims, organisational objectives, performance objectives and learning outcomes (objectives).

Completed (date and sign)..

4.6 Set some clear organisational objectives for a set of outcomes.

Completed (date and sign)..

4.7 Identify correctly the learning levels required according to Bloom's Taxonomy.

Completed (date and sign)..

4.8 Set some specific performance objectives for given examples.

Completed (date and sign)..

4.9 Devise some learning outcomes for a given case study using Robert Mager's PCS framework.

Completed (date and sign)..

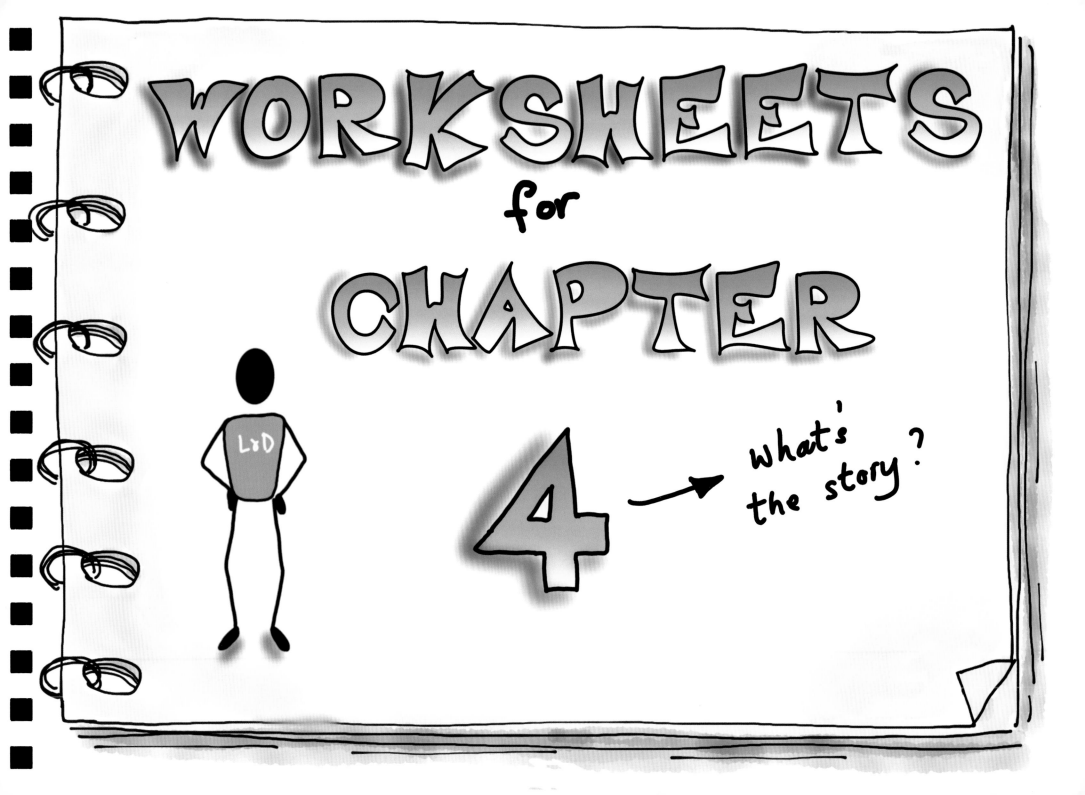

SELECTING WAYS TO PRESENT DATA

Choose 3 different methods and sketch here

How will you draw conclusions?

1
2
3

What are the limitations of these methods?

1
2
3

©Krystyna Gadd 2018

170

4.5 What is it?

Look at the aims/objectives below and determine which of these they might be:

- Aim
- Organisational objective
- Performance objective
- Learning objective

	What is it?
Improve customer satisfaction from 75 to 80% in the 2nd quarter this year.	
To develop communication skills across all teams	
In a role play situation, demonstrate the use of our 5 step complaint handling model with a customer, to an agreed positive outcome.	
Improve personal timekeeping, reducing incidences of lateness from the current level of 4 times per month to once a month by the end of third quarter of this year.	
Cut employee absence from 22% to 15% by 3Q	
Using the dummy system correctly update your weekly absence figures	
Help employees to become aware of the absence management system and how to use it	
Reduce absence in your team down to the company limit of 15% by 3Q	

4.5 The Answers

	What is it?
Improve customer satisfaction from 75 to 80% in the 2nd quarter this year.	Organisational objective
To develop communication skills across all teams	Aim
In a role play situation, demonstrate the use of our 5 step complaint handling model with a customer, to an agreed positive outcome.	Learning objective
Improve personal timekeeping, reducing incidences of lateness from the current level of 4 times per month to once a month by the end of third quarter of this year.	Performance objective
Cut employee absence from 22% to 15% by 3Q	Organisational objective
Using the dummy system correctly update your weekly absence figures	Learning objective
Help employees to become aware of the absence management system and how to use it	Aim
Reduce absence in your team down to the company limit of 15% by 3Q	Performance objective

4.6 Writing Organisational Objectives

Let us imagine that you have just finished an analysis and you now need to develop some organisational objectives from these outcomes:

1. Mistakes in the budgeting system are frequent and it means that line managers are not accurately predicting the budgets that are required annually for their teams. The shortfall at times is up to 10% which means that forecasting cash flow is difficult

2. Recruitment costs have slowly been rising over the years. Last year costs went up by 13%. Attrition rates are also on the rise. Last year the attrition rate was 19% and this year it was 20.5%

3. You have lost 3 major customers and your customer satisfaction score has fallen from 83% to 78%. The number of customer complaints has risen from 23 per month to 36 in the last 6 months alone

Create some organisational outcomes that will help you stay focussed on what the organisation needs.

4.6 Writing Organisational Objectives – the answers

1. All team budgets forecast to be accurate within 2% annually

2.
    i)   Attrition annually to be reduced from 20.5% to 18% by 3Q
    ii) Recruitment costs to increase in line with inflation in the coming year

3.
    iii) In the coming year, to retain all existing class 1 customers and to recruit 2 more
    iv) To improve the customer satisfaction score to 80% by 2Q, 82% 3Q and 83% by 4Q
    v) To reduce the monthly complaints from 36 per month to 20 by 4Q

4.7 Blooms Case Studies

This is a visual of Blooms taxonomy a great way to determine what type of learning is needed and at what level. For the case studies, firstly decide is a knowledge, skills or attitude thing? Then look at the appropriate domain to see which level. The examples in the second visual may help.

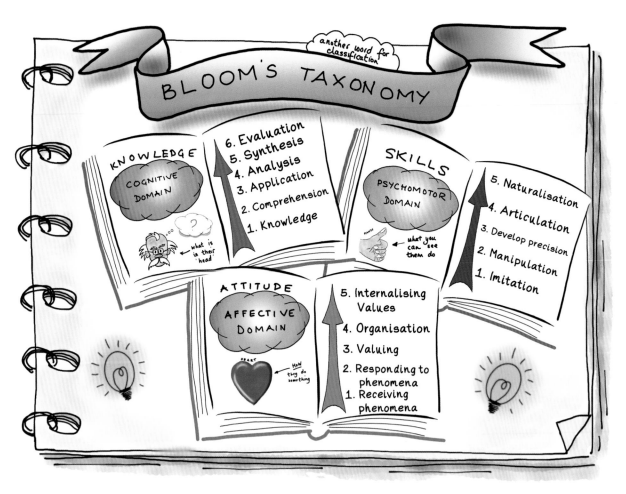

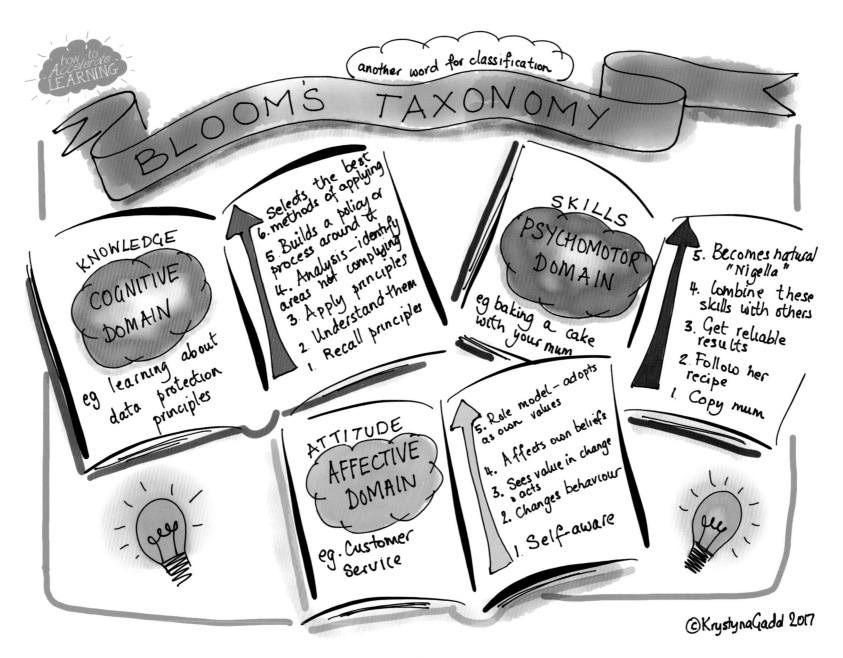

177

Customer service team member behaves according to the 7-step customer service charter.

Learners can use an excel spreadsheet consistently to create meaningful graphs.

Your learners have to be able to calculate an employee's holiday entitlement.

A team of managers have to be able to put together a budget for their department and justify it to the board.

Team leader has to become an expert in dealing with customer complaints regardless of the situation.

Answers

Customer service team member behaves according to the 7-step customer service charter.

Affective Responding

Learners can use an excel spreadsheet consistently to create meaningful graphs.

Psychomotor Develop Precision

Your learners have to be able to calculate an employee's holiday entitlement.

Cognitive Application

A team of managers have to be able to put together a budget for their department and justify it to the board.

Cognitive Evaluation

Team leader has to become an expert in dealing with customer complaints regardless of the situation.

Psychomotor Naturalisation

179

4.8 & 4.9 Identifying & Setting Great Objectives

1. Look at the objectives below and according to Robert Magers' framework, which components do these objectives have?

Objective	P?	C?	S?
Describe 5 characteristics of the customer service excellence model			
Explain the Kouzes and Posner Leadership model, without reference to notes			
List the data protection principles correctly			
Write 3 learning objectives with the use of notes, using Robert Magers' PCS Framework			

ANSWERS

Objective	P?	C?	S?
Describe 5 characteristics of the customer service excellence model.	√	x	√
Explain the Kouzes and Posner Leadership model, without reference to notes	√	√	√
List the data protection principles correctly	√	x	√
Write 3 learning objectives with the use of notes, using Robert Magers' PCS Framework	√	√	√

2. You are the line manager of the individuals below and now need to write you some performance objectives for the following scenarios:

Your learners have to be able to calculate an employee's holiday entitlement.
Learners can use an excel spreadsheet consistently to create meaningful graphs.
Customer service team member behaves according to the 7 step customer service charter.
An expert in dealing with customer complaints regardless of the situation.
A team of managers have to be able to put together a budget for their department and justify it to the board.

ANSWERS

Your learners have to be able to calculate an employee's holiday entitlement.
Using the online guidance accurately and with no guidance calculate an employee's holiday entitlement in 10 minutes or under
Learners can use an excel spreadsheet consistently to create meaningful graphs.
Use excel with no supervision to produce the 6 graphs required for our weekly meeting in an hour or less
Customer service team member behaves according to the 7-step customer service charter.
In random observations by your team leader, using the standard CS observation form, at all times be adhering to the 7-step CS charter
An expert in dealing with customer complaints regardless of the situation.
When dealing with customer complaints, these are dealt with according to the guidelines, in a timely manner and with a maximum of one escalation per month
A team of managers have to be able to put together a budget for their department and justify it to the board.
Complete the annual budget for your team, on time and with a maximum of 1 amendment before acceptance.

3. For the following scenario set some learning objectives:

Aim: For managers to be able to give effective feedback to improve performance

Performance objectives:

- To reduce the number of performance improvement plans from 6 to 1 per year
- To increase productivity by 5% annually
- To increase employee engagement from 75% to 80% in a year

Knowledge: Two feedback models
Describe.....
List......
Skills: Giving effective feedback to staff
Conduct.....
Behaviour: Adopt the models, practice them and tell others about the benefits of using them
Advocate....

ANSWERS

Knowledge: Two feedback models
Describe accurately 2 feedback models and their application without reference to notes
List at least 5 benefits of using effective feedback skills, for the team and the organisation

Skills: Giving effective feedback to staff
Conduct an effective* 1-2-1 meeting in a role play situation, giving feedback using one of two models
*use an observation sheet to judge if it is effective

Behaviour: Adopt the models, practice them and tell others about the benefits of using them
Advocate the use of regular and effective feedback to your peers, in the development of their team performance.

Conclusion

When I set out to write this book, it was with the intention of preventing you as an L&D professional from wasting your money on training that is not needed. By taking the mystery and fear out of data analysis, I hope that you now feel equipped to not only analyse learners' needs before any learning takes place, but also that the way to do it has been clearly laid out. The activities and case study were put together to demonstrate that in analysing the data, you get a clearer view of how to improve performance through transformative learning.

I hope you enjoy the journey and have great stories to share.

About the Author

Krystyna Gadd has been in the field of learning and development for over 30 years. She is a consummate professional with a passion for helping people perform better through learning. She is a member of the CIPD and has delivered professional CIPD L&D qualifications. She is also a fellow of the Learning and Performance Institute.

With her background as an engineer, Krystyna applies the same process thinking to L&D as she did in her former career. Having moved from engineering to IT training, she spent years learning her craft firstly for IBM and later as a freelance IT trainer. This gave her great insight into how to make dry and technical training more dynamic and impactful.

A move into soft skills training in 2003 led Krystyna to research accelerated learning. She was particularly drawn to how learning could become more engaging as well as impactful. A frustration with the many models and theories within accelerated learning prompted her to create a signature system 'Five Secrets of Accelerated Learning', which simplifies all relevant theories and models for those curious about accelerating learning through their organisations.

Krystyna's focus is always on achieving business results in a creative and inspiring way. Through Five Secrets, she helps people make this structured and simple. A curious mind drives her to seek new innovations and consider how the latest research can be applied. She is a pragmatist with a thirst for learning and sharing with others, with the ultimate aim to elevate the L&D profession. Finding the right data to inform good decision-making is a must in her eyes.

Since 2008, Krystyna has been training trainers. Noticing a lack of experience and skill in the area of needs analysis drove her to write this book *How to Not Waste Your Money on Training*.

If you have enjoyed this book and want to know about Krystyna and How to Accelerate Learning then check out her website www. howtoacceleratelearning.co.uk for resources, courses and other events. Read her articles (2016 and 2013) on the Five Secrets of Accelerated Learning to see how you might further revolutionise your L&D department.

Get in touch to find out how she could help you revolutionise your L&D function.

Krystyna Gadd
krystyna@howtoacceleratelearning.co.uk, @KrystynaGadd

References

1. *Driving the New Learning Organisation*, Daly, J. and Overton, L. 2017. Towards Maturity
2. *The Fifth Discipline,* Senge, P. 1990. RandomHouse
3. *Treating Learning Content as a Strategic Business Asset*, Rider, K. 2018. Talent Development
4. *Employee Training and Development (Fourth Edition),* Noe, R. 2008. McGraw-Hill
5. *Learning Analytics,* Mattox, J., van Buren, M. and Martin, J. 2016. Kogan Page
6. *Five Whys and a Why Not,* Fogle, A. and Kandler, E. 2017. Quality Progress. Vol 50, Iss 1
7. *Start with Why,* Sinek, S. 2012. Portfolio
8. *Map It,* Moore, C. 2017. Montesa Press
9. *How to Be a True Business Partner*, Harrison, N. 2008. Nigel Harrison
10. *Driving Performance and Productivity,* Ahmetaj, G. and Daly, J. 2018. Towards Maturity
11. *Stakeholder Mapping, Proceedings of the Second International Conference on Information Systems,* Mendelow, A. 1991. cited in *Exploring Corporate Strategy*, Johnson, G. and Scholes, K. 2002. Financial Times Prentice Hall
12. *Learning Need Analysis and Evaluation (Second Edition),* Bee, F. and Bee, R. 2003. CIPD
13. *Mixing Qualitative and Quantitative Methods: Triangulation in Action,* Dick, TJ. 1979. Administrative Science Quarterly
14. *Fresh Thinking in Learning and Development: Part 3 of 3, Insight and Intuition,* Prof. Smith, E. with Dr McGurk, J. 2014. CIPD
15. *Managing Information and Statistics,* Bee, F. and Bee, R. 2005. CIPD
16. *Quick Off the Mark,* Gadd, K. 2013. Training Journal
17. *Get Up to Speed,* Gadd, K. 2016. Training Journal
18. Learning and Development Practice, Beevers, K. and Rea, A. 2010. CIPD
19. https://www.trainingzone.co.uk/lead/strategy/becoming-an-ld-data-detective-how-to-collect-facts-before-you-start-training Kevin M Yates Training Zone November 9th 2018
20. *Learning & Development,* Rosemary Harrison, 2008 CIPD
21. *Preparing instructional Objectives,* Robert F. Mager 1984, Lake Publishing

Appendix A

LNA Methods

Level of analysis	Name of method	Description	Qualitative or Quantitative?
Organisational	360 feedback	Collect views and opinions from: • People senior to you • Your peers • Anyone who reports to you. Use an online system to collect and analyse data from the organisation. It should have the capability to produce overall, departmental and individual reports.	
	Analysis of corporate mission and strategic plans	Look at the strategic direction of the company and what is important: the goals, vision and mission. This gives a good idea of the 'ideal' you are heading for.	
	Analysis of performance reviews	Only possible to use this efficiently on an organisation-wide basis if the recording method is online and the software has reporting capabilities. Checking to see the percentage of individual/departmental objectives have been met is an important part of this method.	
	Critical incident Technique	Following an organisation-impacting event, follow up and investigate to uncover the underlying causes. Ensure that non-learning causes are considered.	

	Focus groups	Gather opinions from a wide variety of people at different levels spread across the organisation. Use carefully selected questions, without bias and ones where the answers can be collated and drawn together to give some quantitative conclusions.	
	Implementation of projects	Set a clearly defined project with strong objectives and measures. Put in place methods to get affirming and adjusting feedback for the project members. The project measures could be about how quickly/efficiently the project was implemented. This would also reflect on the teams/ departments involved.	
	Records checking – complaints, MI, waste	Check over existing metrics that are collected and engage with the stakeholders that collect it. Endeavour to get pre- and post- measures to assess the impact of the learning interventions.	
	SWOT	Strengths Weaknesses Opportunities Threats Collect responses and thoughts from a wide range of people from the organisation in different positions to get a more balanced view. If you can get an independent facilitator to facilitate and record the answers, it means everyone can get involved who needs to be. It can identify current and future requirements.	
Departmental	360 feedback	Collect views and opinions from: • People senior to you • Your peers • Anyone who reports to you. Use an online system to collect and analyse data from the organisation. It should have the capability to produce overall, departmental and individual reports.	

	Analysis of performance reviews	Consider how you might use the data to inform you of what is happening in terms of developmental gaps, how you can make the data as quantitative as possible to give a good feel for the state of the organisation. Checking to see if departmental objectives have been met is an important part of this method.	
	Analysis of departmental plans	Look at the metrics in the plans to decide which are the most important. This will inform you of the priorities and what should be measured as part of the evaluation.	
	Competency framework	If used as part of the appraisal process, these can assess how competent the department or individuals are in comparison to what they need to be.	
	Critical incident technique	Following an organisation-impacting incident, you could identify key departments to see where there may be gaps in performance.	
	Focus group	In a large department, a selection of team members may be brought together to collect their opinions. You can still devise questions that indicate what percentage of the team are feeling positive about this or that aspect. A focus group could also be used to gauge customer opinions on a specific department.	
	Implementation of projects	Set a clearly defined project with strong objectives and measures. Put in place methods to get affirming and adjusting feedback for the project members.	
	Interview team	Be intentional and clear in the outcomes you want from the interviews (as it may be part of a critical incident investigation perhaps) so that the data you collect can inform decisions on how to improve performance.	
	Quality checks	This should be readily available and it is worth checking with stakeholders which checks are most important. It's a great method to use as it requires little effort if already happening.	

	Questionnaires	Often over-used as a method for analysing needs. For more than a few people, an online questionnaire will be easier to administer. Online survey systems, allowing a variety of different types of questions to avoid user complacency, can be insightful and stimulating to complete.	
	SWOT	Strengths Weaknesses Opportunities Threats As a team activity, this could help bonding, as well as identifying issues. In a divided team, it may be wise to allow moments of quiet reflection and the use of sticky notes so that each voice is heard.	
Individual	360 feedback	If the department is not too big, this can be done on paper, but requires someone to collate and analyse the data. If you use an online system and it has the capability to produce individual reports, this will be very simple to collect.	
	Analysis of performance reviews	For an individual, this can be an easy way to assess the developmental gaps that exist, as long as feedback is honest, kind and backed up with clear examples. Checking to see if individual objectives have been met are an important part of this method.	
	Assessment centre	This is a great way to assess the gaps of employees or suitability of prospective ones. A variety of knowledge and skills activities will give some quantitative data, whereas group activities, observing interaction and leadership qualities will give some qualitative data.	
	Hierarchical task analysis	This breaks down a task into a series of steps in order that you can analyse where there may be difficulties or gaps.	

	Identification of own needs	With a well-structured questionnaire, using a mixture of scaled and open questions, an individual could easily assess their own needs.	
	Interviews	Be intentional and clear in the outcomes you want from the interviews so that the data you collect can inform decisions on how to improve performance.	
	Job analysis	Using an individual's job specification, person specification and feedback on their actual role, a job analysis can identify the knowledge, skills and behaviours required for an individual and also any current performance gaps.	
	Observation	Using a well-formed observation sheet, this does not always have to be carried out by an expert in the field. As long as the activities or outputs to be observed are well-defined, the observer can use the sheet as a guide to score an individual's performance.	
	Quality checks	Little effort required if these are already set up as part of a manufacturing process or system – sampling calls, for instance, in a call centre.	
	Questionnaires	This is often over-used as a method for analysing needs and can be tedious if using a manual approach. Online survey systems, allowing a variety of different types of questions to avoid user complacency, can be insightful and stimulating to complete.	
	Scoring grid	As part of a job analysis, you could use a scoring grid (also known as a skills matrix) to either score the individual yourself or allow them to self-score. The latter would have to be checked by another opinion.	

	SWOT	Strengths Weaknesses Opportunities Threats This can be done as an individual exercise with input from others. It could help structure a line manager conversation with a team member and include valuable feedback.	
	Testing	Formal tests can be part of any approach where you are looking to determine developmental gaps. A pre-set scoring guide will help maintain consistency.	
	Work sampling	Work sampling with strict assessment criteria will be a good way to gauge an individual's ability to achieve the standards required in their work and any development necessary. It is most likely to be performed by a supervisor of some kind. Most suited to work where something is produced that can be sampled.	
Job role	Focus group	A selection of team members may be brought together to collect their opinions on a new or existing role.	
	Hierarchical task analysis	This breaks down a task into a series of steps in order that you can analyse where there may be difficulties or gaps that require support.	
	Job analysis	Using a job specification and a person specification, a job analysis can identify the knowledge, skills and behaviours required for an individual coming into a role.	

	Manpower planning	Planning resources required for a team or department may lead to new job roles being created or old ones being adjusted. If new roles are created, it may require development that has not been required in the past.	
	Succession planning	This may be part of a wider talent or leadership programme, where needs are identified.	
	SWOT	Strengths Weaknesses Opportunities Threats This can be done as a group or individual exercise with input from others for a new or existing role.	

Appendix B

The New Learning Leader

We help organisations, line managers, teams and individuals to:

- Have a strategic outlook when considering how people will learn to improve performance
- Learn how to engage with stakeholders and leverage them when looking for support and resources
- Be curious and dig deeper on underlying issues to find out what is needed
- Choose a complementary blend of opportunities to help people improve their performance (#100ways2learn)
- Use accelerated learning principles so that the learning is 'sticky'
- Be agile and fast
- Use a facilitative approach when doing any learning interventions rather than traditional trainer-led methods
- Build a cohesive learning community that benefits the whole organisation
- Open up to new ways of doing things
- Be motivated and inspired enough to have a go

Our open and in-house workshops do much more than 'train' in the skills and knowledge required to become a trainer. We are preparing to become new learning leaders for the new learning organisations.
Through unique and innovative practices, we have seen teams:

- Have a mindset shift in their thinking about how they approach learning
- Become more cohesive in their approach to improving performance
- Be inspired to make a real and measurable difference to the organisation by helping people learn how to improve their performance

To compliment the 'New Learning Organisation', we have developed our second draft on the **New Learning Leader:**

The visual is above but the detail is below:

1. Has clarity of purpose and is performance focussed, not training or technology lead
   - Business-focused but also learner-centred
   - Strategically focused to deliver what the organisation needs
   - Curious and analytical
   - Able to engage stakeholders in order to leverage essential resources and achieve the ROI required
   - In tune with what the organisation needs
2. Helps create a holistic people experience
   - Helps to nurture and encourage an environment where people are developed consistently and with heart
   - Clearly defined and easy-to-apply models and frameworks
3. Supports and nurtures a thriving ecosystem
   - Knows how to encourage a learning culture
   - Inspires a culture of feedback and healthy challenge
   - Empowers people to learn for themselves
   - In learning interventions, inspires others to learn more and share
   - Promotes accountability at all levels
4. Agile, digitally enabled
   - Digitally courageous, not scared to experiment
   - Able to choose the appropriate method/media for the outcomes required
5. Helps support continual engagement
   - Provides appropriate learning support when it is needed
   - Understands the way the brain works to help learning be engaging and focused
6. Helps people make intelligent decisions
   - Makes decisions informed by the organisation's purpose and finds the data to support it
   - Develops others' capability in decision-making by providing the appropriate tools and collecting the right data
7. Emotionally intelligent self-starter
   - Has awareness of their own behaviours on others
   - In touch with their own emotions
   - Good networker
   - Loves to learn

Appendix C

100 Ways to Learn

Action learning sets	Brainstorming	Drama played out by actors	Job enlargement	Object lesson	Q&A session	Skills practice	Watch a demonstration
Activity de-brief	Breakout sessions	DVD	Job rotation	Observation	Quality circle	Special interest group	Watch a presentation
Analogy	Buddying	E-learning	Job share	Business balls,Trainer bubble websites etc	Quiz	Storytelling	Webinar
Appraisal review	Cards/laminates	Facilitated discussion	Join a forum	On-the-job	Quotations	Surf the net	White board exercise
Apps for mobile devices	Case studies	Fill in the blank questions	Learn from mistakes	Peer feedback	Read a book	Syndicate groups	Wordsearch
Ask for feedback	Charades	Find a buddy	LinkedIn	Photos and images	Reflect on performance	Teach back	Workbooks
Ask the expert	Coaching	Flashcards	Mentoring	Physical walk through a process	Research	Team Coaching	Workshops
Attend a lecture	Collaborate on a piece of work	Flipchart exercise	Mobile – search engine	Pictionary	Review a piece of work	TED talk	Write an article
Attend a meeting	Collage of ideas from magazine pictures	Flipchart walk around	Mind maps or flow charts	Podcasts	Role play	Television programme	YouTube
Attend a professional meeting	Conference	Formal teaching session	Models/props	Posters	Scavenger hunt	Trial and error	
Attend a seminar	Delegation	Games	MOOC	Professional qualification	Search or discovery	Twitter	
Attend a training course	Discussion	Hand outs	Mood boards	Professional journal	Secondment	Use of metaphors	
Board game	Draw a picture	Icebreaker	Networking	Project work	Simulation	Walk and talk	

Appendix D

Voices on Learning Needs Analysis

John Swallow, Head of L&D, Specsavers CREATE

In 2016, a decision was made to change the campaign strategy across the region. After reviewing the potential impact on the customer experience, it was further decided to support this with a training program to help our store team members explain the enhanced customer offer. We would also use this opportunity to define, train and embed behaviours to elevate our customer service.

Following discussions with key stakeholders, clear objectives were defined, and a cross-functional project team was established. Then, analysis was done on the behaviours that would be needed to achieve this and what the potential gap was, together with research on what our best people were already doing that could be shared. The CREATE program was born. Originally launched in our Australian business, this was a training program that focused on the key behaviours of: Coach, Relate, Enquire, Adapt, Teach and Engage, together with a unique theme that everyone could get behind. In Europe, we were able to adjust and re-focus the program to our specific needs.

In order not to reinvent the wheel, we gathered together all the relevant materials that we could find. Following a deep dive into these to find the most useful materials, we overlaid our requirement and developed a blended program involving seminars, classroom events, virtual classroom, webinars, videos and an interactive self-reflection tool.

The program was launched in spring 2017 and trained thousands of store team members across the region, utilising virtual training, group seminars and regional events where possible to enable cost-effective delivery and comprehensive engagement. By working closely within a project team, we also received strong board and other functional support, which helped with participation and engagement across the business.

The overall result of the campaign change was an uplift in customer volume, a higher uptake on the focus KPI for the campaign and an overall increase in customer satisfaction. The high engagement in CREATE also enabled us to continue to include it within our future L&D strategy. Results were communicated and a review took place to define how it could be designed and delivered even better next time.

Had we not undertaken the learning needs analysis at the beginning of the process, which determined such clear objectives, we would not have been able to deliver on these to the extent that we did. Also, of great benefit was global sharing, stakeholder involvement and being able to answer the critical question 'why?' to achieve strong engagement of store teams.

Michelle Dunn, Group Learning, Knowledge and Readiness Manager, Lowell Group

Everyone assumes we share common definitions and meanings and it's only through completing a thorough needs analysis that you can establish what your customer really wants. I've found that sometimes this process helps the customer think through and challenge their own requirements. By moving away from vague statements, you can establish the specifics expected and create tangible results.

At every point of the design, delivery and measures, it felt like the goalposts were moving and I had no reference points to go back to. Having no documented agreements turned a 'simple' task into months of work and rework. Never again!!

Emma Shaw, independent consultant

I was invited to an initial consultation with a social housing provider who said they were looking for a couple of days' training on customer excellence for their contact centre. I happily accepted and discovered in that meeting that their needs actually came from a core issue around culture, geographical disconnect and a breakdown in internal communication process.

I used questioning to uncover this quite quickly. Had I taken what they perceived as their needs at face value, I would have been at risk of designing and delivering a programme that didn't deliver results, perhaps would not engage the people involved and actually would not have been worth their investment.

As things turned out, the business in question didn't proceed any further with this enquiry as they felt they had other more pressing priorities. However, I would rather this than risk my reputation as a learning provider, and waste their financial investment and time on something that would not solve a problem for them in the long term. Sticking plasters are all well and good, but being a true consultant often means that you have to highlight some harsh truths for people; if they are unable to assimilate this in some way, it may mean that you don't win their business as a result.

A client I worked with for around nine months brought me in to support the learning and development aspects of a major project affecting the core and corporate functions of their business in a significant, business-critical way. This would involve huge change for their colleagues as well as systems and process change. Part of the reason I was brought in was to support this change and mindset element.

I conducted a thorough needs analysis and got right under the skin of the business very quickly, getting immersed in their culture and really understanding their challenges and strengths.

What followed was a frustrating few months where I spent a good many hours, days and weeks writing business cases and having myriad meetings to attempt to get the approval for the change activities they greatly needed – in other words, they were paying me handsomely to spend time trying to get them to allow me to facilitate the activity I was procured to deliver in the first place!

Ultimately, it became apparent to me that I was unable to support them to do what they needed to do as the nature of the business and those in the upper echelons of the organisation were just too blinkered and overwhelmed to see that a fundamental and dramatic transformation in their culture and people engagement was needed for them to achieve their goals.

We parted ways. Around three months later, news was announced that sadly they would be going into administration. I often wonder what could have happened had I got in earlier and they'd had a number of positive influences to help them understand the danger ahead.

Nathan Dring, independent consultant
Huge fan of gut feel. Love the *Blink* principle by Malcolm Gladwell, which might be because I am more like that, and the idea he calls 'top skimming', when you get a strong idea of which way to go without listening to all the information. All that said, being able to back up gut feel with some science adds a huge amount of credibility. When you blend the two, I think you are your most authentic self.

Question on LinkedIn:

Gathering top tips for my book on *How to Not Waste your Money on Training*, what is your top tip that you would share with others? Have you used this yourself?

Jacci Wright
Before assuming that a gap requires training to fill it, ask those with the gap what would be the best way for them to bridge that gap. You'll be amazed how often they don't say training. When I do a training needs analysis, I always ask this question and find that often the bridge is either a communication, coaching or operational issue that needs addressing.

Eric Linin, Head of Talent Development, The Corporation of Lloyd's
Targeted coaching for leaders often removes the need for remedial training for their team.

Owen Ashby, Head of Strategic Alliances and Engagement
I'd assess first to evidence the gap, then only ask learners to invest time in the learning they actually need, then post-assess to evidence you've closed the gap.

Cathy Hoy (FLPI), Director and Founder, Learning Bar
Stretch yourself to really think about what you can create for 'free'. Work with enthusiastic SMEs in the business, up-skill line managers to better embed any formal learning so it's not wasted. Also, make sure any learning intervention is properly aligned to the strategic direction of the business!

Tom Grand
I would begin with what you are trying to achieve: warm and fluffy or change?

Martin Baines, The Sales Training Specialist
Ensure buy-in from managers or business leaders. If they aren't bought in, there won't be any support when learners return to work and therefore an unlikelihood of any behavioural change. Involvement and buy-in at both pre- and post-learning stages.

Linda Fell, Owner, Premium Virtual Assistance Ltd and Associate, The Hoxby Collective
Make sure that the trainer knows their stuff. How long have they been teaching their subject? Get testimonials from people who have been on their courses.

Gareth Evans MSc, Organisational Development
Look through the lenses of the business problem not the perceived training or learning solution in the first instance.

Sean Riordan, Learning and Development leader

Stop. Step back. Ask why. What's wrong or not working? Ask why again. Get to the root cause, understand the symptoms and issues. Ensure that the manager and MOR (manager once removed) is involved. Get to fully understand the mechanics of the issues and how L&D can assist performance. Make sure that everyone knows that we are not magical and cannot fix everything; some things are within the culture and not easily corrected.

Jackie Handy (FIRP)

Be sure the leaders of the business are involved at LNA stage, know what training is being delivered and why, and commit to supporting team members 'post-workshop'. Training is not just a stand-alone magic wand. It needs commitment from the whole business to embed and build upon. That's where the true ROI lies. "The fish rots at the head".

Lee McDonald, learning and development organisational development specialist

Fix the right gap by doing a decent NA. Stop 'sheep dipping'.

Annie B, Mabo B

Learn as you go.

Responses from Twitter:

Marie Duncan, L&D manager

Ask probing questions about the need for the training before arranging. Explore alternatives to training. Assess what change you are looking for as a result of the training and measure that.

Kevin Maye

Keep asking 'what do we want to change?' and 'why isn't that already happening?' The answer might be training but more likely some other task aid.